Macmillan Education
4 Crinan Street
London N1 9XW
A division of Macmillan Publishers Limited
Companies and representatives throughout the world

ISBN 978-1-4050-5878-0

Text © Mary Bowen and Printha Ellis 1998 and 2004
Design and illustration © Macmillan Publishers Limited 2004

First published 1998
This edition published 2004

All rights reserved; no part of this publication may be
reproduced, stored in a retrieval system, transmitted in any
form, or by any means, electronic, mechanical, photocopying,
recording, or otherwise, without the prior written permission
of the publishers.

Illustrated by Dave Woodroffe

Cover design by Andrew Oliver
Cover illustration by Pencil and Pepper

Printed and bound in India

2018
20 19 18

1

1 Write the words in the puzzle.

2 Write answers to the questions.

1 What does Emma's father do?

_____

2 Where is he now?

_____

3 Who is in the bank?

_____

4 What does Jill's father do?

_____

5 Where is he going?

_____

6 What is he going to do?

_____

Unit 1 Lesson 1 **3**

1 Look, find and write.

Where are they going to go? How are they going to go there?

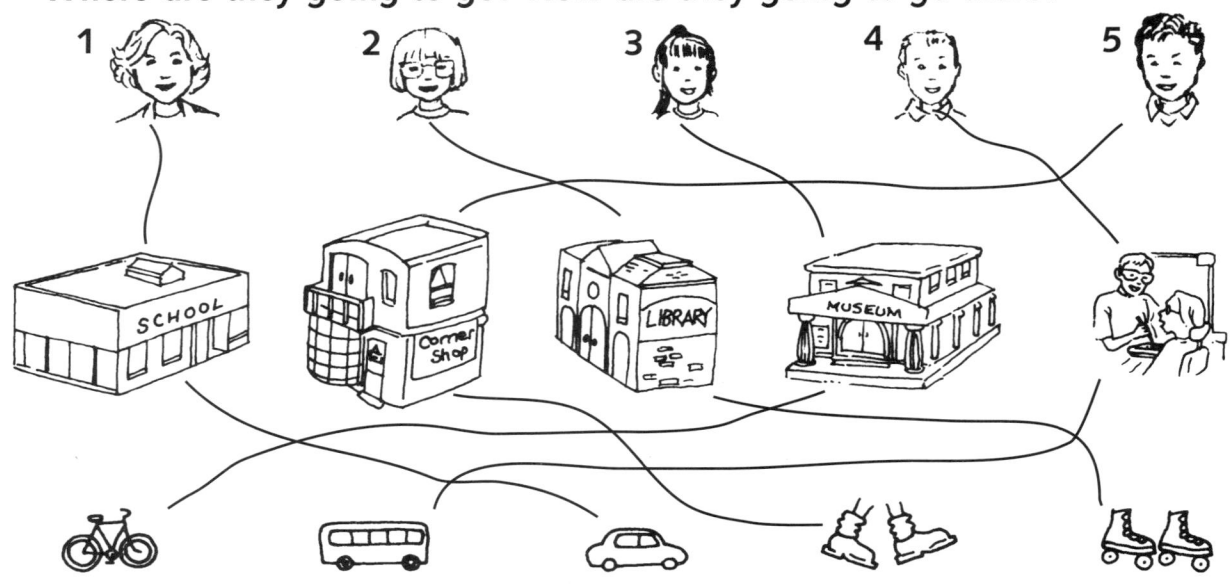

Mrs Hill's going to go to school. She's going to go by car.

 Emma

 Jill

 Ned

Sam

2 Write the answers. Use the sentences in the box.

Yes, I do.	No, I don't.

1 Do you go to school by bus?
2 Do you go to the library on foot?
3 Do you go to the dentist by car?
4 Do you go to the park on roller blades?
5 Do you go to the shops on your bike?

Unit 1   Lesson 2

1 Complete the sentences about the library.

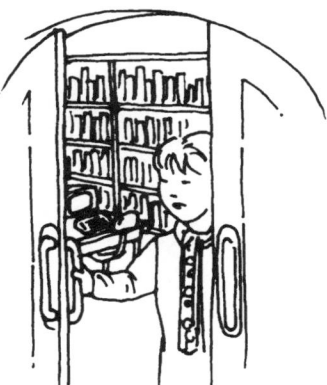

CLIFTON LIBRARY: HOURS
Open: Tuesday, Wednesday, Friday
Closed: Monday, Thursday, Saturday, Sunday

1 The library is always open _on Tuesday, Wednesday and Friday._
2 The library is never open _____
3 The library is never closed _____

2 Complete the sentences about the dentist. Use the words in the box.

Dentist
Hours of work
Monday – Friday
9 am – 12 pm
2 pm – 6 pm
Saturday (Winter only)
9 am – 2 pm

1 The dentist _____ works on Monday morning.
2 The dentist _____ works on Sunday.
3 The dentist _____ works on Saturday.
4 The dentist _____ works until 6 pm.

sometimes
often
always
never

3 Write four sentences about yourself.

1 I always _____
2 I often _____
3 I usually _____
4 I never _____

Unit 1   Lesson 3

1 Sue is going to go to the swimming pool.
Match the people with where they are going to go.

1. Peter
2. Lily
3. Sue
4. Bob
5. Shelley
6. Gary

2 Write a sentence about each person.

1. _____
2. _____
3. _____
4. _____
5. _____
6. _____

3 Where are you going to go on these four days?
Write four sentences.

1. On Monday _____
2. _____
3. _____
4. _____

Unit 1   Lesson 4

Composition

1 Look at the picture. Write the questions next to the answers.

What is he going to do?
Who is this?
How old is he?
Why?
What is his name?

_____ This is Susie's older brother.

_____ His name is Bill.

_____ He's 16 years old.

_____ He's going to be an animal doctor …

_____ … because he really loves animals.

2 Write about the picture. Use the questions about Bill and the words in the box to help you.

thirteen
Lily
cousin
librarian

I'm Kitty and this is Lily.

_____
_____
_____
_____
_____

Unit 1   Composition

Study skills

1 Spelling.
Fill in the missing letters.

__ __ nk   __ __ nk   __ __ nk   __ __ nk

Fill in the missing words.

I _____ I'll go to the _____.

I stand at the _____ and _____.

Which word does not rhyme?

think   thank   sink   wink   _____

bank   thank   tank   pink   _____

2 Find the odd one out.

1 library   computer   book   car   read   _____
2 reporter   newspaper   shop   write photo   _____
3 dentist   tree   teeth   clean brush   _____
4 bread   cakes   meat   baker biscuits   _____
5 police   uniform   car   station fish   _____
6 matches   sew   needle thread tailor   _____

3 Use , . ? and capital letters.

1 can you see mrs hill   yes i can
2 where are you going next monday   to school

Unit 1   Study Skills

2

1 Look at the picture and answer the questions about Clifton in 1600. Use the words in the box.

> Yes, there was.   No, there wasn't.   Yes, there were.   No, there weren't.

1 Were there any buses? _____
2 Was there a river? _____
3 Were there any shoes? _____
4 Were there any horses? _____
5 Was there a supermarket? _____

2 Answer the questions about people in Clifton in 1600.

Where did they live?

The prince _____
_____

Who made these?

1 _____ made _____ .
2 _____ made _____ .
3 _____ made _____ .

Unit 2   Lesson 1

1 Complete the words. Then circle them in the puzzle.

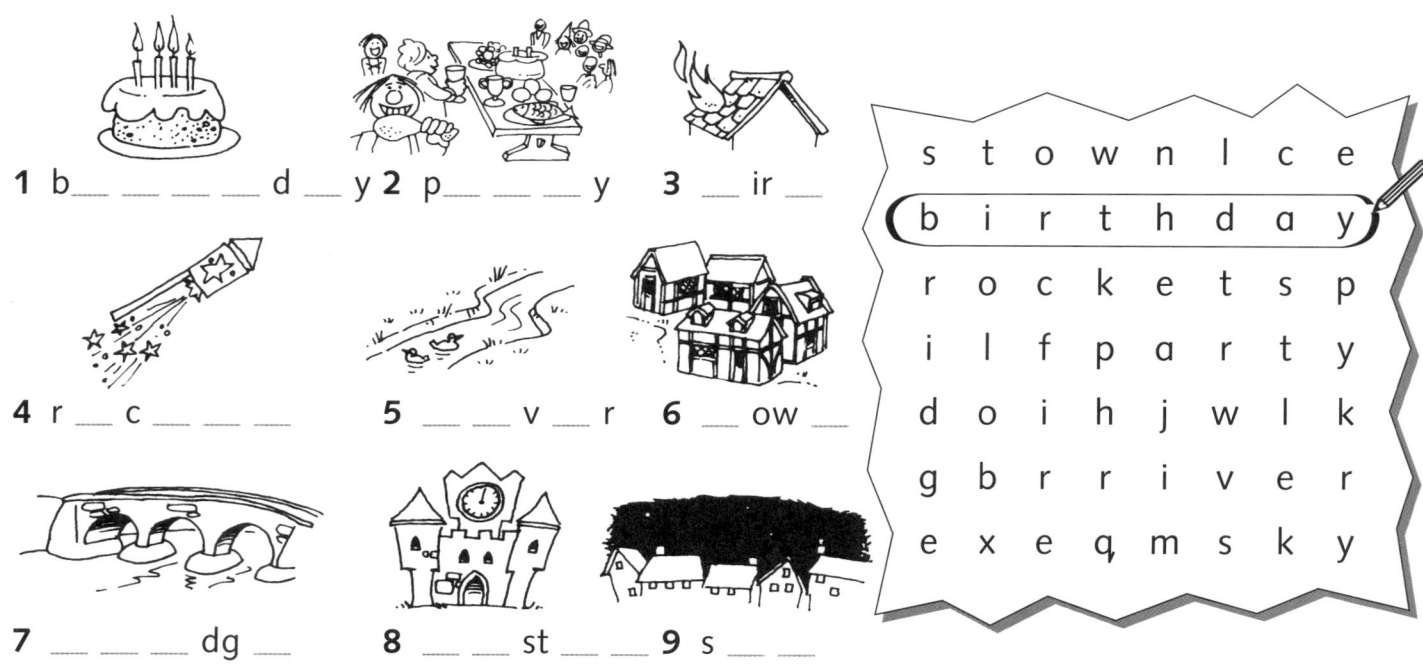

1 b__ d__y 2 p__y 3 __ir__
4 r__c__ 5 __v__r 6 __ow__
7 __dg__ 8 __st__ 9 s__

2 What did they do?

Write a sentence about each picture.

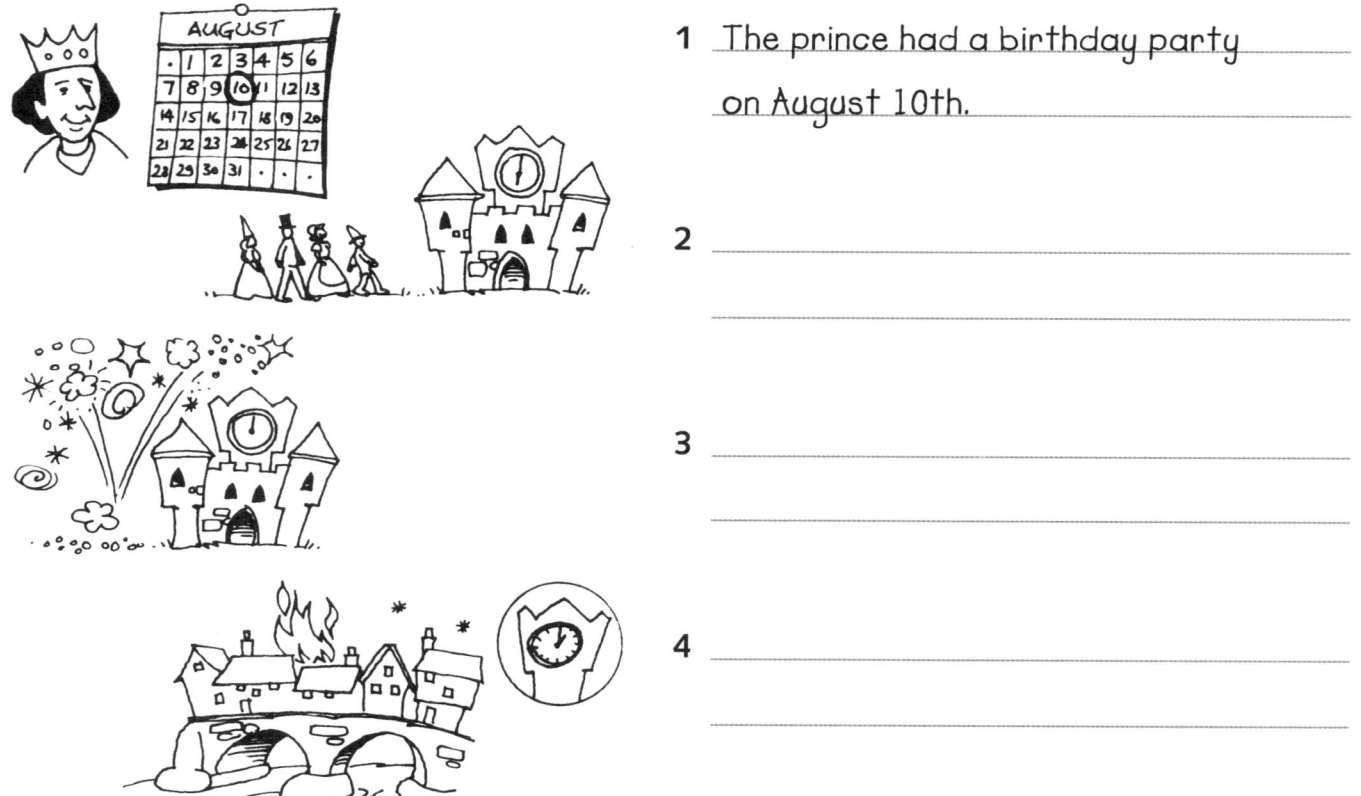

1 The prince had a birthday party on August 10th.

2

3

4

Unit 2   Lesson 2

1 Write sentences about the pictures. Use the words in the box.

| big | young | small | clean | fast | slow | dirty | wide | narrow | old |

1   The castle is bigger than the house.
2   The shop is smaller than the house.

3   _____
4   _____

5   _____
6   _____

7   _____
8   _____

9   _____
10 _____

2 Draw and write. Where did you go yesterday? Draw a picture. Write a sentence about it.

Unit 2   Lesson 3

1 Read.

Susan went to Scotney Castle with her aunt and uncle. The castle is in England. It is 700 years old. There is water around the castle.

Nobody lives in the castle now. Some of the walls are falling down. Susan saw how the people lived in the past. She saw where they slept and where they ate.

Susan and her uncle liked visiting the castle very much. Susan's aunt did not like it. 'It's boring,' she said.

2 Write answers.

1 Which castle did Susan visit?

2 Where is the castle?

3 How old is the castle?

4 Who did Susan go with?

5 Who lives in the castle?

6 Who liked visiting the castle?

Composition

1 Jack and Jane had birthday parties. Read about Jack's party, circle the date and draw the times in the clocks. Then number the pictures.

Jack had a birthday party on Tuesday, July 4th. Jack and his friends went to the cinema at 3.30. Then they all went back to Jack's house at 5.00. At 5.30 they had dinner. And they played games at 6.15. They had a wonderful time!

2 Look at the pictures of Jane's birthday and draw the times. Then write a story.

Unit 2   Composition

Study skills

1 Spelling.

Fill in the missing letters.

sh _u_ _t_   sh ___ ___   sh ___ ___   sh ___ ___

sh ___ ___ ___   sh ___ ___ ___ ___ ___   sh ___ ___ ___ ___ ___

Fill in the missing words.

A _____ wearing _____ .   A _____ on a _____ .

2 Write these words in alphabetical order.

shop   ship   sheep   shoe

1 _____

butcher   baker   bread   butter

2 _____

cook   chocolate   cake   carrots

3 _____

market   meat   man   men

4 _____

3

1 What would they like?

1 Jack would like some crisps.

2 _____

3 _____

4 _____

5 _____

6 _____

2 What do they say to the shopkeeper?

1 Jack says, 'I'd like some crisps, please.'

2 Mrs Hill says, 'Please can I have _____'

3 Emma says, 'I'd _____'

4 Ned says, 'Can _____'

5 Becky says, 'Can _____'

6 Jill says, 'I'd _____'

1 Answer the questions.

crisps 30p
colouring book 75p
roses 99p
chocolates £3
newspaper 50p
cola 45p

1 Jack has 60p.

Can he buy some crisps? _____

Can he buy some crisps and a cola? _____

2 The policeman has £4.

Can he buy some chocolates? _____

Can he buy chocolates and roses? _____

3 Becky has £1.20. What can she buy?
_____

4 Jack's dad has 80p. What can he buy?
_____

2 What does the shopkeeper say?

1 How much are the crisps? *They're thirty pence.*

2 How much is the cola? *It's forty-five pence.*

3 How much are the roses? _____

4 How much are the chocolates? _____

5 How much is the colouring book? _____

6 How much is the newspaper? _____

Unit 3   Lesson 2

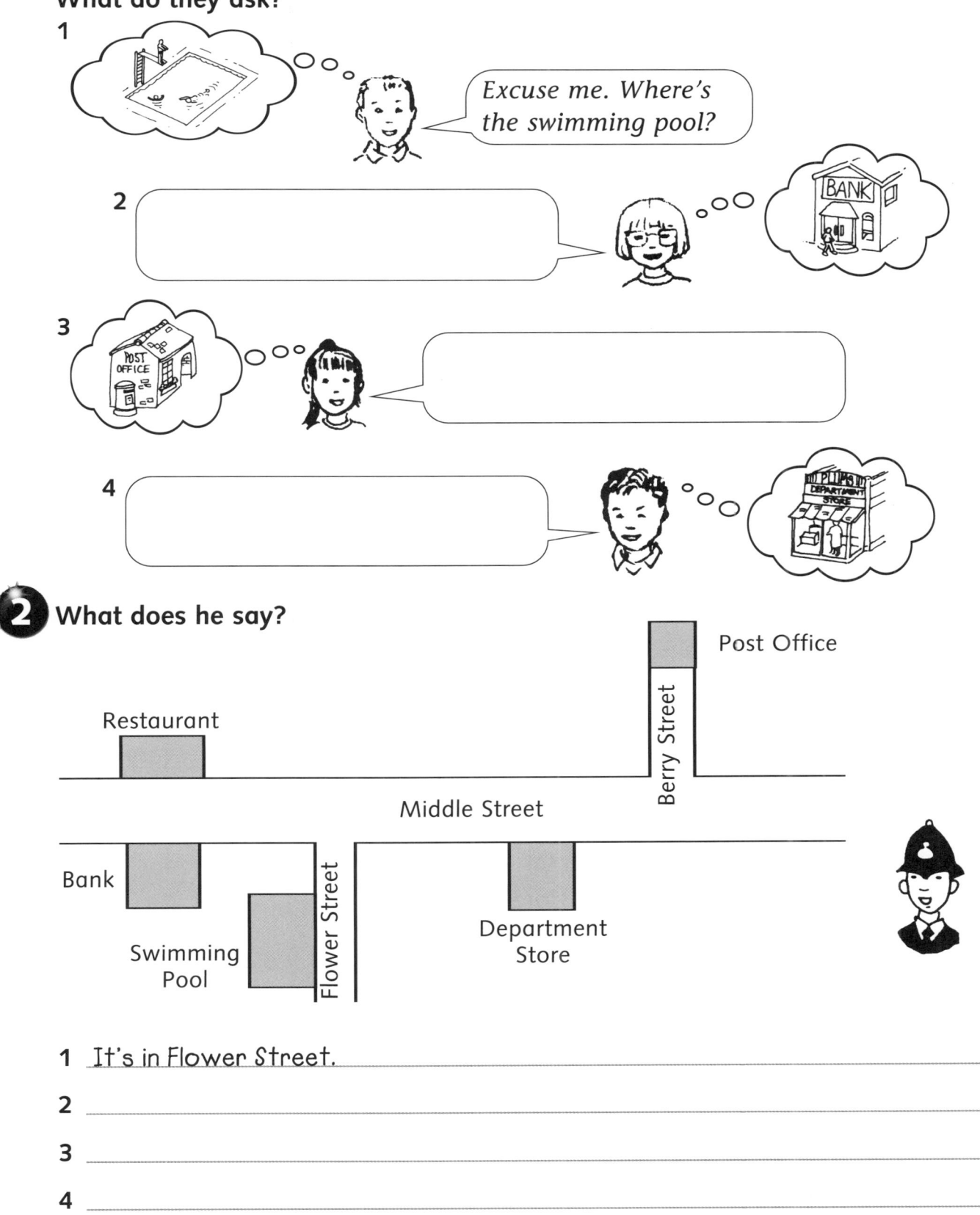

1 What do they ask?

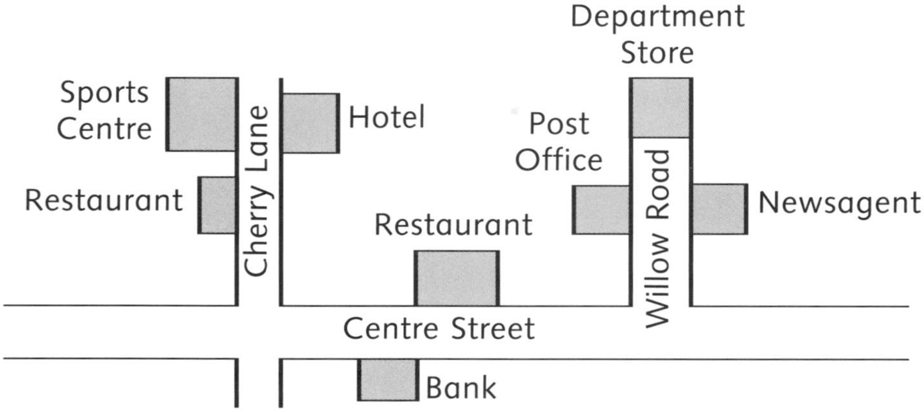

Excuse me. Where's the bank?
Go along Centre Street. It's on the left.

_____?
It's opposite the sports centre.

_____?
It's at the end of Willow Road.

_____?
It's on Cherry Lane, next to the restaurant.

_____?
It's opposite the post office.

2 Read and write the names.

This is Twintown. It has a lot of nice buildings. Begin at the bank. Go straight on. There is a post office on the right. Turn right at Market Street. There is a department store on the left, and opposite the department store is the library. Go straight on and turn left. You are on Station Road. There is a hotel on the right and there is a restaurant next to the hotel. The railway station is at the end of the street.

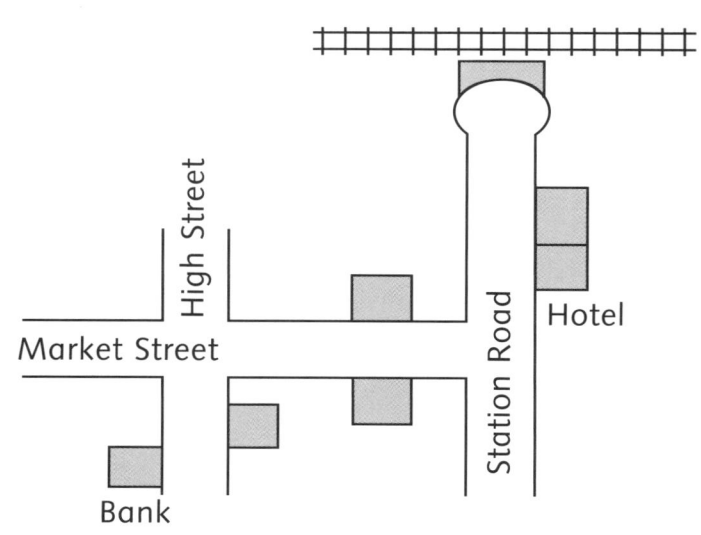

Composition

1 Sarah's story. Read the story and write the numbers under the pictures. Answer the question.

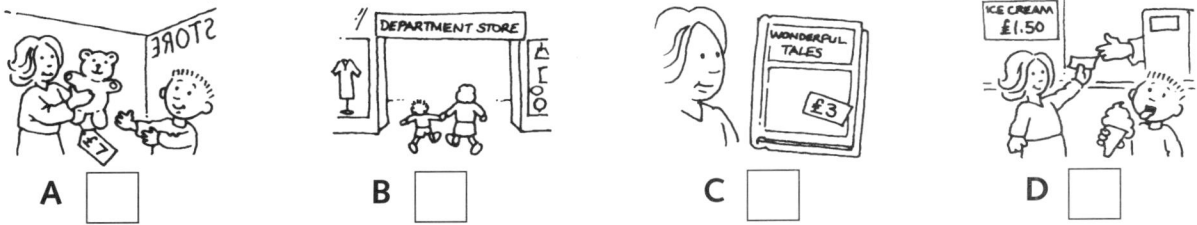

£7

A ☐

DEPARTMENT STORE

B ☐

WONDERFUL TALES
£3

C ☐

ICE CREAM £1.50

D ☐

It's Saturday. Sarah goes to a big department store with her brother Larry. She has £12. First they go to the toy department. Larry wants a teddy. It's £7. Next they go to the restaurant. Larry wants an ice cream. It's £1.50. Then they go to the book department. Sarah wants a story book. It's £3. Can Sarah buy the story book?

2 Mr Smith's story. Write about Mr Smith. Use the words in the box.

First	Next	Then	Can Mr Smith buy ...?

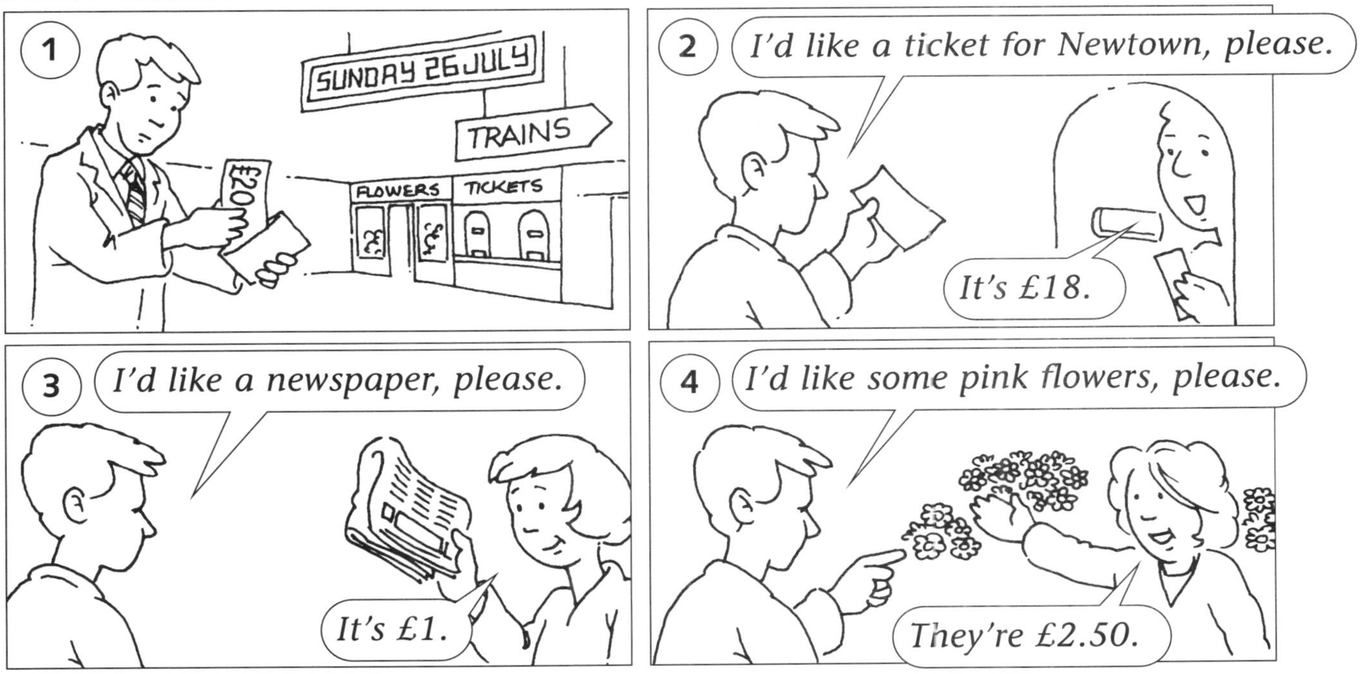
1
SUNDAY 26 JULY
TRAINS
£20
FLOWERS
TICKETS
2
I'd like a ticket for Newtown, please.
It's £18.
3
I'd like a newspaper, please.
It's £1.
4
I'd like some pink flowers, please.
They're £2.50.

Study skills

1 Spelling.
Fill in the missing letters.

1 Wh __ __ is your name?
2 Wh __ __ do you go to the park?
3 Wh __ __ is your birthday?
4 Wh __ __ do you do on Saturday?
5 Wh __ __ __ do you live?
6 Wh __ __ __ does your father work?
7 Wh __ won the race?
8 Wh __ did you go by train?
9 Wh __ are you crying?
10 Wh __ went with you?

2 Write questions for these answers. Remember the ?

1 _____

My name is Sarah.

2 _____

I live in South Street.

3 _____

My birthday is on Saturday.

4 _____

Because I feel sad.

5 _____

The boy in the blue shirt.

6 _____

He works at the market.

1 Look at the pictures in the box. Then find the words in the puzzle.

2 Answer the questions.

1 Can I paint the wall?  Yes, but you must wear an apron.

2 Can I play outside?  Yes, but you must wear

3 Can I go to the party?

4 Can I go to the mountains?

5 Can I go to the shop?

Unit 4   Lesson 1

1 Look and write. Write 'must' or 'mustn't'.

1 Can I cut the string? Yes, but you __must__ be careful!

2 Can I make a cake? Yes, but you _____ wear an apron.

3 Can I hold the baby? Yes, but you _____ drop her.

4 Can I cook some soup? Yes, but you _____ touch the stove.

2 Write sentences.

1 Can I ride my bike? Yes, but you must wear shoes.

2 Can I play outside? _____

3 Can I cut the bread? _____

3 How does Jill make a clown puppet?
Look and write. Use the words in the box.

| next | first | after that | finally |

Jill is making a clown puppet. First, she _____

_____

_____

_____

22 Unit 4 Lesson 2

Composition

1 Read and ✔. This is how to make a cake.

You must have a bowl ... a spoon ... and a baking tin. You must have sugar ... and butter ... an egg ... and some flour, ... and you must have an oven.

2 Write the recipe and draw your cake. Use the words in the box.

| sugar butter add egg stir flour bowl mix tin bake oven |

(cake) _____

Study skills

1 Spelling.

Say these words. The <u>a</u> has a short sound.

Sam   can   tap   hat   cap

Say these words. The <u>a</u> has a long sound.

same   cane   tape   hate   cape

Complete the sentences. Use the words in the boxes.

1 | Sam / same | _____ doesn't look the _____ as Ned.

2 | hat / hate | I _____ this _____!

3 | cap / cape | You wear a _____ on your head and a _____ around your shoulders.

2 Put these books in alphabetical order. Write the numbers 1–6 in the boxes.

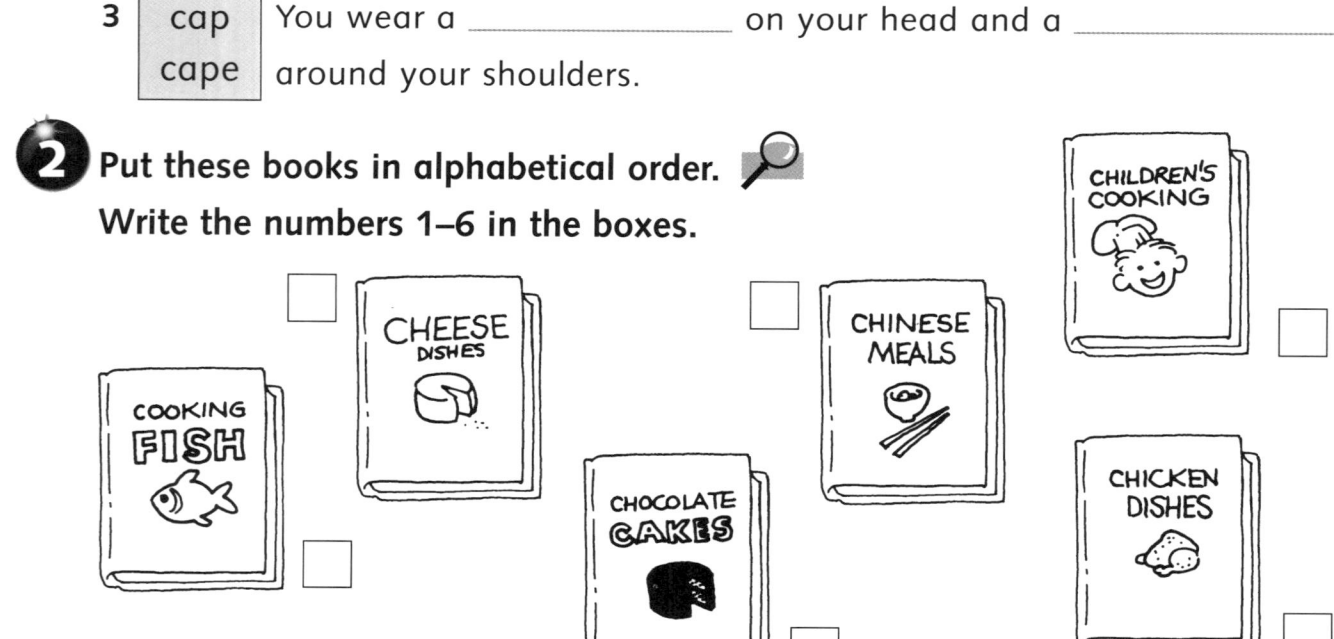

Unit 4   Study Skills

Revision

1 What are they going to do?

1
2
3
4

2 Answer the questions.

Last week Emma and Becky were on holiday.

1 Where were they?

2 What did they do?

3 Who was on the beach?

4 What was in the harbour?

5 What was in the sky?

3 Write sentences.

Say what you must/mustn't do.

1
2
3

4 What are they saying?

1. Would you _____ ? Yes, _____
2. Can _____ ? Yes, of _____
3. _____ would you _____ ? I'd _____

5 What are they saying? Use the words in the box.

| give | show | read | me | us | them |

1. Please _____ a story.
2. _____ the photo.
3. You mustn't _____ any nuts.

6 Look at the pictures. Write the sentences (use the words in the box).

| gives it to the postman | writes a letter |
| writes his friend's name | puts it in an envelope |

First _____ After that _____
Next _____ Then _____

7 Write the sentences.

1. Now he _____ in a house.
   Before he _____ in a flat.

2. Last year there _____ any hotels.
   This year there _____ two.

Unit 4 Revision continued

1 Look at the pictures of things at a pleasure palace. Write the words.

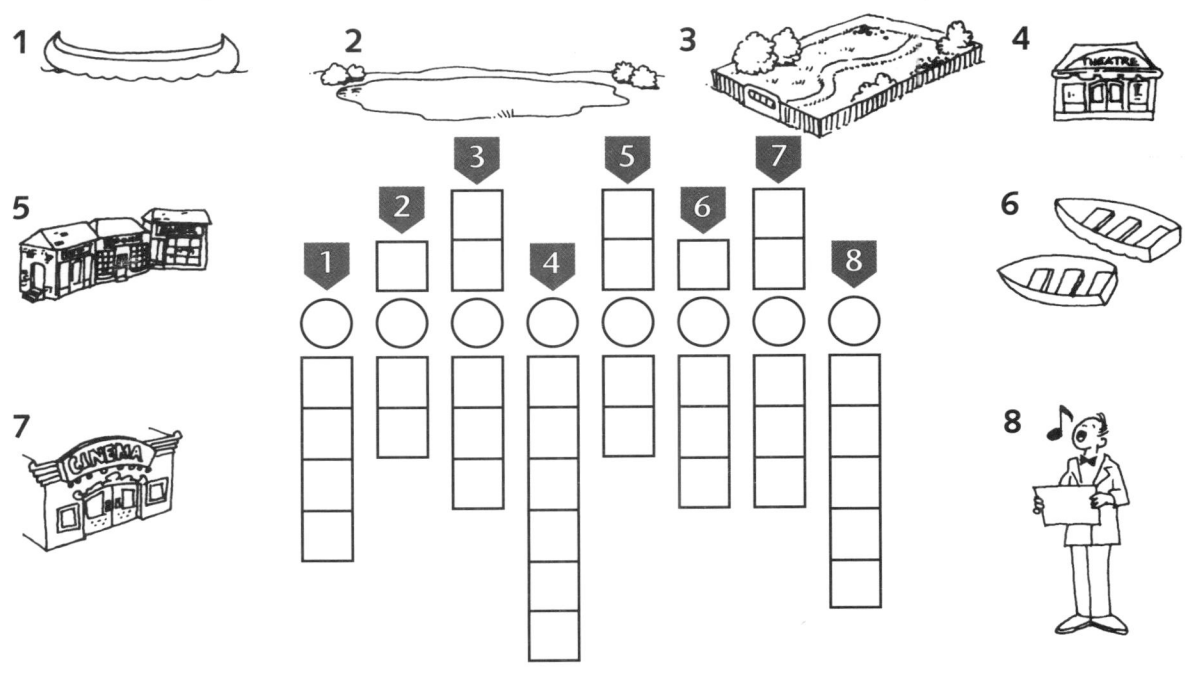

Bob and Bill are going to the cinema. What will they see?

Look at the letters in the circles and ✔ the picture.

2 Write a short article about the Merryland Hotel.

> The new
> **Merryland Hotel**
> will have everything!
> ★ shops ★ restaurants
> ★ garden with
> ★ swimming pool ★ tennis court
> *Kiko the clown will open the hotel at 12 o'clock on Saturday 14th July.*

The new Merryland Hotel will _____

_____

_____

_____

_____

_____

Unit 5   Lesson 1

1 Write the answers and the questions.

1 What's this for? It's for _____

2 What are these for? They're for _____

3 What are these for? _____

4 What's this for? _____

5 _____ They're for _____

6 _____ _____

2 What are they saying?

1 Shall we play tennis?
   Yes, let's!

2  Shall we go trampolining?
   No, let's go _____

3  Let's _____
   _____

4 _____
   _____

5 _____
   _____

Unit 5   Lesson 2

1 Write answers.

1 What will the weather be like tomorrow?

   It will be hot and sunny tomorrow.

2 What will the weather be like next week?

___

3 What will the weather be like next month?

___

4 What will the weather be like next week?

___

5 What will the weather be like tomorrow?

___

6 What will the weather be like next month?

___

2 Look and write.

| in the north |
| in the south |
| in the west |
| in the east |

Write 4 sentences about tomorrow's weather on Penny Island.
Use the words in the box.

___
___
___
___

Unit 5   Lesson 3   29

1 Read the text and look at the pictures. Circle the mistakes.

Peter will go on holiday with his family in July. They will go to Scotland in the United Kingdom. They will travel by train.

The weather will be hot and sunny. Peter will see snow for the first time. His mother will buy him a warm coat and some boots in Scotland.

Peter will have lots of fun with his family in Scotland. They will visit a museum, and they will sail a boat on a river. Peter will send postcards to his friends at home.

2 Write the sentences correctly.

_____
_____
_____
_____
_____
_____

3 Yes or No? ✔ the box.

	Yes	No
Peter and his family live in Scotland.	☐	☐
They will visit the United Kingdom in January.	☐	☐
The weather will be cold.	☐	☐
Peter's mother will buy him new clothes.	☐	☐
Peter will sail in a canoe.	☐	☐

Composition

1 Read, find and write the number.

Read this newspaper article.

Sunny Saturday, says coach.

There will be an important football game at the Carling Football Pitch on Saturday 30th May. The Bears will play the Lions and the game will start at 2.30. Tickets will be £5 for adults and £3 for children. You can buy them at the gate. 'The weather will be good. It will be hot and sunny,' says the coach.

Find these things in the text and number the boxes.

time   place   tickets   weather   teams   date
☐   ☐   ☐   ☐   ☐   ☐

2 Read, look and write an article.

Read the poster and take notes on the notepads below.

Don't forget!
Friday 3rd August, 7 o'clock

Dolphins v Penguins

play basketball at Essex School

Tickets on sale at the door
£7/£5

Use the numbers in the boxes to help you write your article.

Study skills

1 Spelling.
Fill in the missing letters.

st a l k   t _ _ _   ch _ _ _   w _ _ _

Which word does not rhyme?

talk   chalk   stalk   ask   _____

board   boat   lord   cord   _____

Make words from these letters.

m e n i c a    d o y l u c    r h a e t e t

_____   _____   _____

v i r r e    a l e k    h e e t r a w

_____   _____   _____

2 Match.

1 let's   ( ) we are
2 it's   ( ) did not
3 we'll   ( ) will not
4 I'm   ( ) let us
5 we're   ( ) are not
6 they're   ( ) it is
7 isn't   ( ) I am
8 aren't   ( ) they are
9 doesn't   ( ) do not
10 don't   ( ) we will
11 didn't   ( ) does not
12 won't   ( ) is not

1 Write answers.

1. Should we drink lots of milk? Yes, we should.
2. Should we eat lots of chocolate? _____
3. Should we wash our hands before meals? _____
4. Should we play in the road? _____
5. Should we play with matches? _____
6. Should we brush our teeth twice a day? _____

2 Look at the answers. Write questions.

1. Late for school again!
2. I love vegetables!
3. I go to bed early.
4. Can I help?
5. Too much TV!

1 Should we _____ No, we shouldn't!
2 _____ Yes, we should!
3 _____ Yes, we should!
4 _____ Yes, we should!
5 _____ No, we shouldn't!

Unit 6 Lesson 1 33

1 Write sentences. What does Billy eat?

1 Billy doesn't eat much _____
2 He doesn't eat many _____
3 He eats a lot of _____
_____

2 Write sentences. What does Betty eat?

1 Betty doesn't eat much _____
2 She doesn't eat many _____
3 She eats a lot of _____
_____

3 What do you eat? Finish the sentences.

1 I don't eat much
2 I don't eat many
3 I eat a lot of

1 Finish the sentences. Use the words in the box.

| from side to side | twice a day | twice a year |
| up and down | every three months | |

1. You should visit the dentist _____
2. You should brush your teeth _____
3. You should brush your teeth _____
4. You shouldn't brush your teeth _____
5. You should change your toothbrush _____

2 What should you eat and drink? Write sentences.

1. You should eat a lot of _____
_____
2. You should drink a lot of _____

What shouldn't you eat and drink? Write sentences.

3. You shouldn't eat much _____
4. You shouldn't eat many _____
5. You shouldn't drink much _____

1 Find the words. Write them in the puzzle.

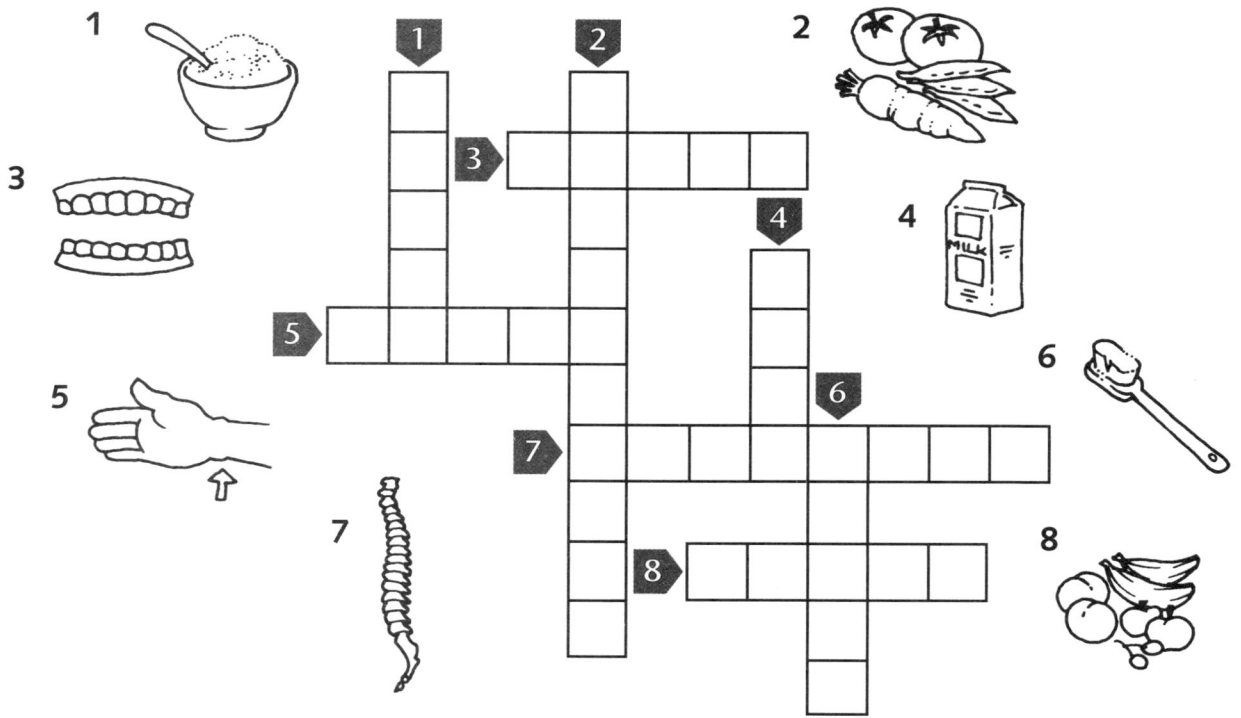

2 Write using the words in the box.

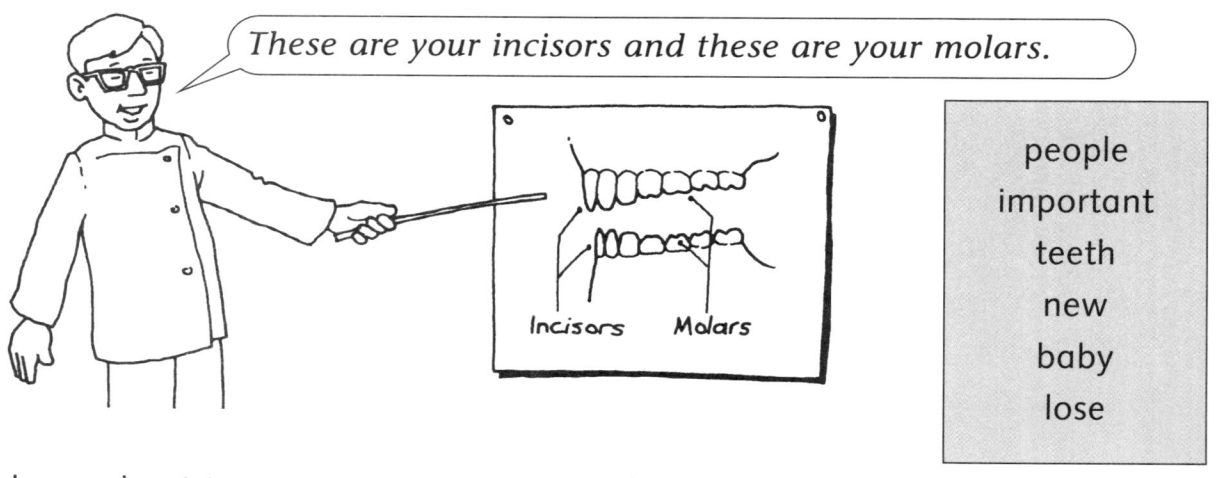

people
important
teeth
new
baby
lose

You have about twenty _____ teeth. These fall out when you are six or seven years old. Then you get _____ teeth. An adult should have thirty-two _____. The large teeth at the back of the mouth are called 'molars'. The sharp teeth at the front are called 'incisors'. Some _____ don't take care of their teeth. Then they _____ them. Your teeth are _____ – take good care of them!

Unit 6   Lesson 4

Composition

1 Look at the pictures of Sally and Joe.

eats a lot of sweets

2 Match the words in the box with the pictures. Make notes.

| brush teeth | eat a lot of … | go to the dentist | happy because |
| have good/bad teeth | drink a lot of … | afraid because |

3 Read about Joe.

Joe eats a lot of sweets. He drinks a lot of cola. When he goes to the dentist he is afraid because he has bad teeth.

Now write about Sally.

Unit 6   Composition   37

Study skills

1 Spelling.
Fill in the missing letters.

ch _e_ _e_ _s_ _e_   ch __ __ __   ch __ __ __   ch __ __ __

Which word does not rhyme?

much	touch	brush	such	_____
fish	which	dish	wish	_____
bees	cheese	please	teeth	_____

2 Whose pencil is this?

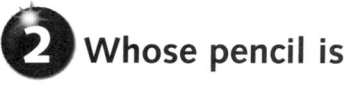 It's mine.

Simon — It's Simon's.
It's his.

Janet — It's _____
_____ hers.

Whose books are these?
They're mine.

Sarah — They are Sarah's.

Bill

Lucy

1 Match the words and the pictures. Write the words for each pair.

A feed	B wash	C sweep	D brush	E water
1	2	3	4	5
brush				
teeth				

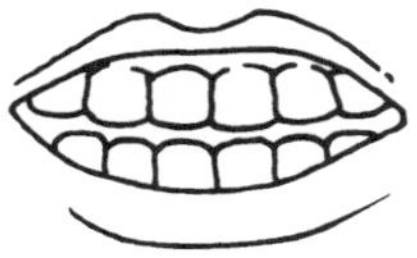

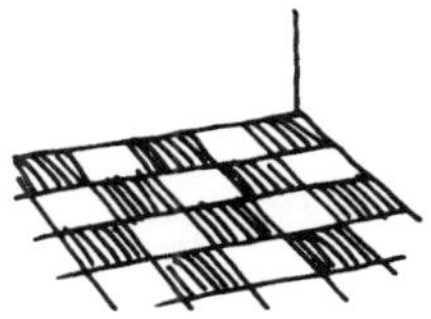

2 Write sentences. Use the words in the box.

| after that   first   then   before bedtime   next |

What does Molly have to do at home?

First Molly has to _____

_____

_____

_____

3 What do you have to do at home? Write a sentence about it.

_____

_____

_____

Unit 7   Lesson 1   39

1 Match then write the letters.

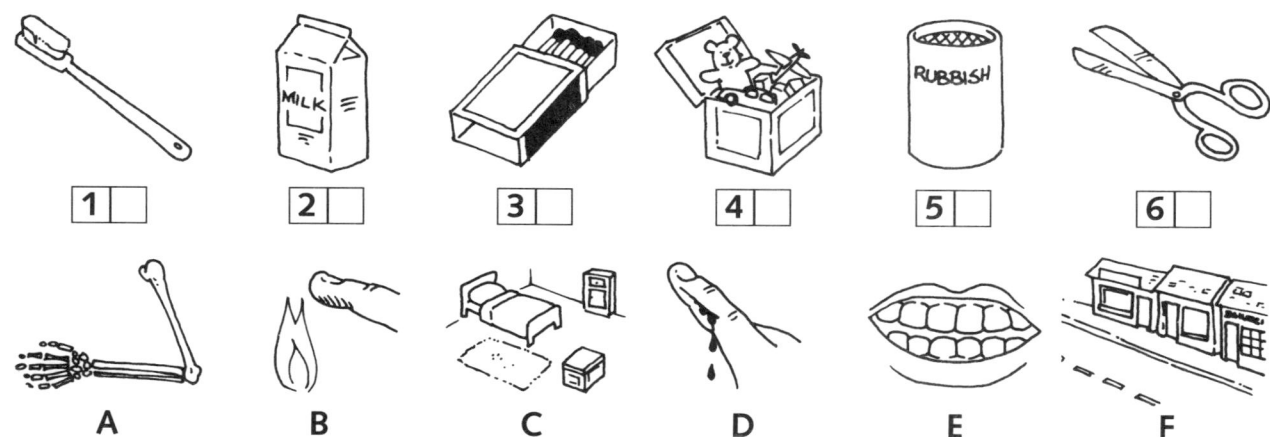

2 Make sentences from this table.

You should	drink lots of milk brush your teeth put rubbish in the bin put your toys away be careful with scissors be careful with matches	so that	your room is tidy. you don't burn yourself. they stay clean. your bones grow strong. you don't cut yourself. your town is clean.

1 You should drink lots of milk so that your bones grow strong.

2 _____

3 _____

4 _____

5 _____

6 _____

3 Write two rules of your classroom.

_____

_____

_____

1 Look at the pictures. ✔ or ✘ the words in the box.

Tod is going on holiday. He's going to the beach.

Katy is going to the mountains for her holiday.

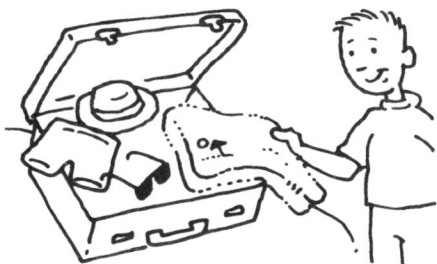 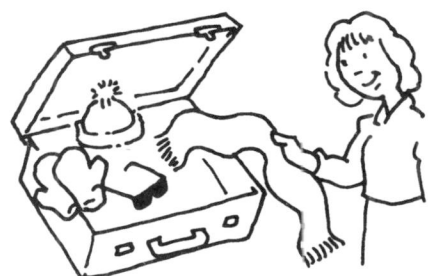

Tod		Katy
✘	gloves	✔
___	hat	___
___	sunglasses	___
___	towel	___
___	scarf	___
___	shorts	___

2 Write sentences.

1 Katy _has to take gloves, but Tod doesn't have to take gloves._

2 Tod _____

3 Katy _____

4 Tod _____

5 Tod and Katy _____

6 Tod and Katy _____

3 Draw and write. You are going on holiday. Draw what you have to take in your suitcase and write about it.

Unit 7   Lesson 3

1 Look and write.

Finish the sentences. Use the words in the box.

> so that you can hear the film.
> so that you don't fall over it.
> so that I can put your food on it.
> so that you don't get hurt.
> so that the plane is tidy.
> so that you sit in the right seat.

1. Please wear a belt _____
2. Please put your bag under your seat _____
3. Look at your seat number _____
4. She will give you some earphones _____
5. Put rubbish in the bin _____
6. Please put your table down _____

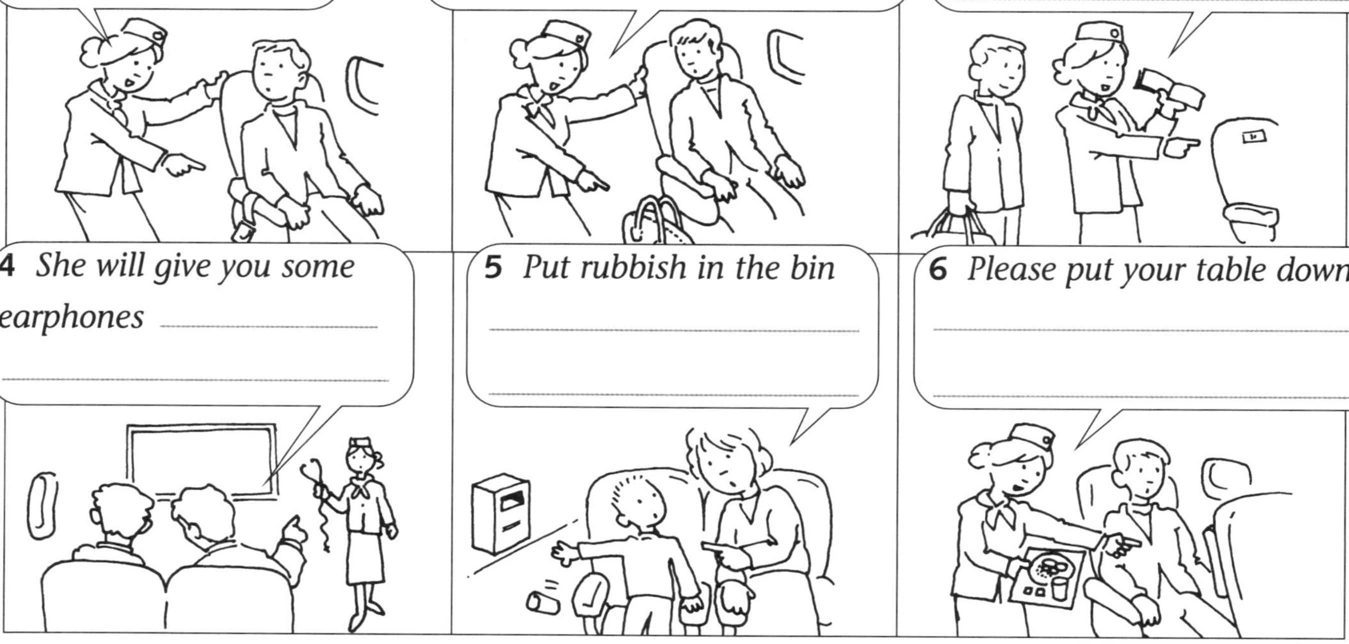

2 ✔ and write.

What do you have to have in your school bag? Why?

I have to have a ruler in my school bag so that I can draw lines.

Unit 7   Lesson 4

Composition

1 Read and write the numbers. Look at Katy's postcard.

What does she write about? Write the numbers.

place   weather   likes   has to   doesn't have to   other people
_____   _____   _____   _____   _____   _____

> Dear Tod
> Here I am in the Blue Mountains. Mum and Dad are here, too. It's very cold and it's snowing. We have to wear boots, jackets, gloves and hats. But we don't have to get up early because it's too cold. We all like the mountains and the snow. See you soon!
> From
> Katy

2 Read and write the numbers.

Tod wants to write a postcard to Katy. Help him put the sentences in the right order. Write the numbers in the boxes.

- ☐ It's very warm and sunny.
- ☐ Hello from Coco Beach.
- ☐ I'm staying with my aunt and my cousin, Fred.
- ☐ But we don't have to wear coats or jackets.
- ☐ I'll be back next week.
- ☐ I really love the sea and the sunshine.
- ☐ We have to wear hats because it's very hot.

3 Now write Tod's postcard.

Unit 7   Composition   43

Study skills

1 Spelling.
Fill in the missing letters.

c r a sh   _ _ sh   _ _ sh   _ _ _ sh

Make words from these letters.

g a b d e a n   c r o s s i s s   t r a s e l p   d o l o b

2 Match.

1 plenty   ( ) a flat dish for food

2 plant   (1) a lot of something

3 plate   ( ) it flies in the sky

4 play   ( ) it grows in the ground

5 please   ( ) you can see it in a theatre

6 plane   ( ) a nice way to ask

3 Write these sentences. Use ? . and capital letters.

1 jack goes to school on monday
2 do we have to take pens
3 in july emma and joe will go to london
4 are there any bears in america

8

1 Look and write. Look at the pencil cases. Write the words.

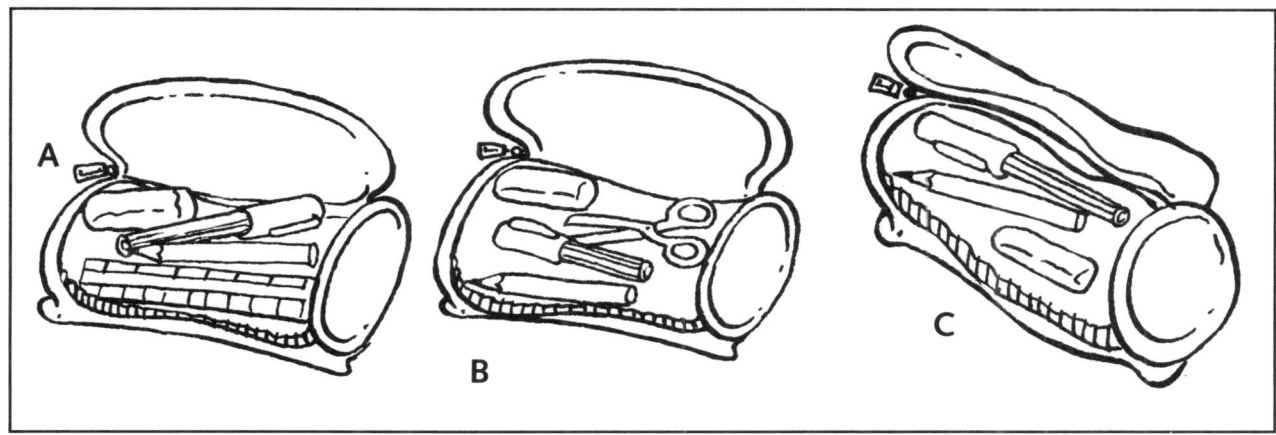

1 Everybody has a _____   2 Somebody has a _____
3 Everybody has a _____   4 Somebody has a _____
5 Everybody has a _____   6 Nobody has a _____

2 Look and write.

Write the answers to the questions. Kim, Nancy and Ben had lunch in a restaurant. What did they have?

Kim   Nancy   Ben

1 Did anybody have a drink?   Yes, everybody did.
2 Did anybody have grapes?   _____
3 Did anybody have soup?   _____
4 Did anybody have a sandwich?   _____
5 Did anybody have crisps?   _____

Unit 8   Lesson 1

1 Match the pictures with the questions. Write the answers.
Use the words in the box.

| usually | sometimes | never |

A B C D E [1]

1 Do you brush your teeth twice a day?
   I always brush my teeth twice a day.

2 Do you eat fruit for lunch?

3 Do you drink milk at night?

4 Do you eat eggs for breakfast?

5 Do you get enough sleep?

2 Look and write about you. Use the words in the box.

1   2   3   4

| every week | ... hours a day | ... hours a night |
| more than once a day | | never |

1
2
3
4

Composition

1 This is Bill's day. Read about it.

```
9.00 – 11.00  Played football      4.00 – 6.00  Read a book
12.30  Had lunch                    6.30  Played with Sally
         (fish and chips)           7.30  Ate dinner (meat, potatoes,
1.30 – 3.00  Watched TV                    salad, ice cream)
3.30  Went for a walk               9.00  Went to bed
```

2 What did Bill do today? Write about it.

Bill played football from 9 to 11. Then he _____

3 Now you. Write five things in your diary for yesterday.

Write about your day.

Unit 8   Composition (lesson 3)   47

Study skills

1 Spelling.
Fill in the missing letters.

sk __

sk __

sk __

__ sk

__ __ sk

(desk image)

__ __ sk

Make words from these letters.

y y d o b r e v e

_____

d o n y o b

_____

m e d y b o s o

_____

s u l y l u a

_____

m i t s o m s e e

_____

v e r n e

_____

2 Write these sentences. Use , ' ' ? and capital letters.

1 the dentist asked do you brush your teeth
   <u>The dentist asked, 'Do you brush your teeth?'</u>

2 the nurse asked what is your name

   _____

3 the fisherman asked do you like fish

   _____

4 the butcher asked do you eat meat

   _____

Revision

1 There will be a new park at Newbridge. Look at the plan. What will there be in the park? What will there not be? Use the words in the box.

| swimming pool | restaurant | boating lake |
| tennis court | puppet theatre | playground |

2 Fill in the missing words.

1 Shall _____ to the museum?
   No, _____ cinema.

2 _____ go to the swimming pool?
   Yes, _____ !

3 Write the answers.
   1 How did Emma feel yesterday? _____.
   2 What did Becky hear yesterday? _____.
   3 What did Ned do on Saturday? _____.

Unit 8   Revision   49

4 Write sentences. Use the words in the box.
What do they eat and drink?

| much | many | a lot of |

1 ✔
2 ✔
3 ✘
4 ✘

5 What are they saying? (Use 'have to' or 'don't have to'.)

1 Be healthy! Eat a lot of cheese. _____.

2 You can stay at home today. _____.
   There's no school.

6 Make three sentences. Choose words from the box.

1 clean your room
2 wash your clothes   so that
3 write words clearly

| tidy |
| clean |
| can read them |

1 _____
2 _____
3 _____

Unit 8   Revision continued

9

1 Read these words. Write the numbers.

| 32,500 | 13,250 | 850,000 | 4,808 | 40,602 |

1 Four thousand eight hundred and eight _____
2 Thirteen thousand two hundred and fifty _____
3 Thirty-two thousand five hundred _____
4 Eight hundred and fifty thousand _____
5 Forty thousand six hundred and two _____

Write the words.

1 500,000 _____
2 14,256   _____
3 84,250   _____

2 Look at the fact file. Answer the questions.

1 Where do gorillas live?
_____

Gorilla

Largest monkey, lives in Africa
Colour: brown or black
Height: up to 175 cm
Weight: 140–180 kg
Eats fruit and vegetables
Sleeps in a tree at night

2 What colour are they?
_____

3 How much do they weigh?
_____

4 How tall are they?
_____

5 What do they eat?
_____

6 Where do they sleep?
_____

Unit 9   Lesson 1   **51**

1 Write sentences. Use 'only a few' or 'only a little'.

1. Once there were lots of whales. Now there are only a few whales.

2. Once there was lots of grass. Now there is

3.

4.

2 Look at the pictures. Answer the questions.

Kerboom!

It was a quiet, hot day in the forest. Bobby was watching a deer and a rabbit. Then …

1. What did the deer do?   It lifted
2. What did the boy smell?
3. What did the rabbit see?
4. What did the fire burn?
5. What did the bear see and hear?
6. Why did the fire stop?
7. Why were the animals happy?

1 Which animal? Read the sentences. Write the letters.

A B

This animal lives in the sea but it is not a fish. (1) ☐ It lived on an island in the Indian Ocean 300 years ago. (2) ☐ It is the largest animal in the world. (3) ☐ Once there were about 220,000 of these animals. (4) ☐ Sailors came to the island and killed all the birds. (5) ☐ This was easy because the birds did not fly. (6) ☐ Men hunted them and today there are very few – only 12,000. (7) ☐ How many are there today? There is not one in the whole world. (8) ☐

2 Write about the dodo or the whale.

_____
_____
_____
_____

3 Read about the animals. Write answers.

Animals in danger

mountain gorilla
1900: 20,000
now: 350

passenger pigeon
1860: 500,000
now: none (0)

1 How many mountain gorillas were there in 1900?
   <u>Twenty thousand.</u>

2 How many passenger pigeons were there in 1860?
   _____

3 How many passenger pigeons are there now?
   _____

4 How many mountain gorillas are there now?
   _____

1 **Read about the animals. Fill in the blanks.**

The gorilla is (1)_____ metres tall, and weighs (2)_____ kilos. The hippo is (3)_____ metres tall, (4)_____ metres long, and weighs (5)_____ tonnes. The elephant is (6)_____ metres tall, (7)_____ metres long, and weighs (8)_____ tonnes.

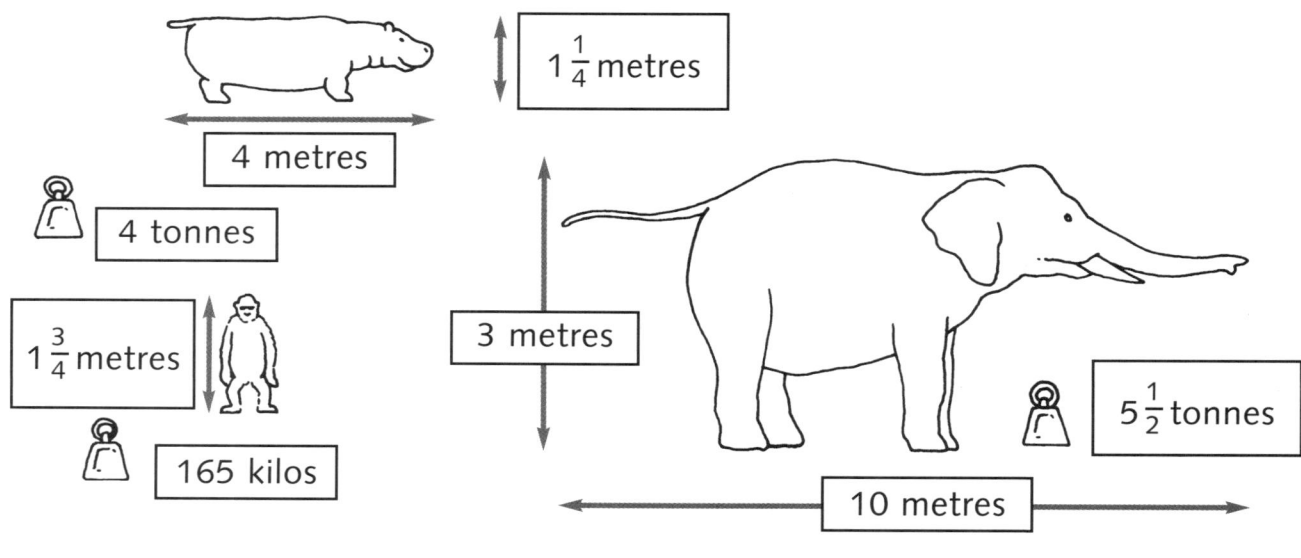

2 **Look at these two dinosaurs.**

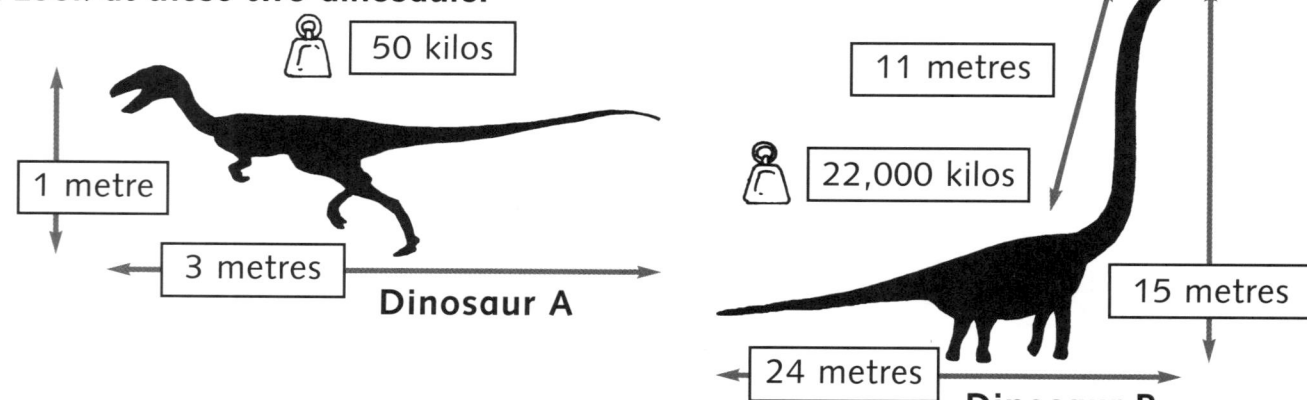

Write answers.

1 How heavy was Dinosaur A? _____

2 How tall was Dinosaur A? _____

3 How long was Dinosaur A? _____

4 How heavy was Dinosaur B? _____

5 How long was Dinosaur B? _____

6 How tall was Dinosaur B? _____

7 How long was Dinosaur B's neck? _____

Unit 9 Lesson 4

Composition

1 Look, find and write. Sally and Sue are at the zoo. Read the description of the bison. Look at the card and fill in the blanks.

Name:	American bison
Lives in:	North America
Coat:	long, shaggy hair
Length:	up to $3\frac{1}{2}$ m
Height:	up to 3 m
Weight:	up to 1,350 kg
Number today:	about 30,000
Food:	grass

American _____

The American bison lives in _____ Its hair is _____ _____ It weighs _____ It is _____ tall and _____ long. It eats _____ There are only about _____ American bison alive today.

2 Write about the blue pike.

Name:	Blue pike
Lives in:	North America
Colour:	blue and grey
Food:	fish and insects
Length:	up to 50 cm
Number today:	none (0)

_____

_____

_____

_____

_____

Study skills

1 Spelling.

Write these numbers as words.

20	30	40	50
w y t t e n	r i h t y t	t y r o f	f f i y t

80	100	1,000
g e y t h i	d h e n u d r	s o u n d h a t

Write these numbers as words.

13 _thirteen monkeys_

500 _____

2,300 _____

11,000 _____

700,000 _____

2 Find the odd one out.

1 camel   blue   red   yellow   green   _____

2 desert   forest   jungle   ocean   book   _____

3 small   long   car   tidy   tall   _____

4 playing   jumping   running   chair   walking   _____

Write a word from each line in the blanks.

This is a picture of a (1) _____ .
It lives in the (2) _____ . The
camel is (3) _____ . It's
(4) _____ .

Unit 9   Study Skills

10

1 Make sentences from this table.

1 You can use ✏️	to clean	🌴
2 People use 🐪	to make	🏠
3 People can use 🪵	to travel	👄
4 People can use 🪵	to eat	🍨
5 We use a 🪥	to build	🔥
6 You use a 🥄	to draw	

1 You can use crayons to draw a picture.
2 _____
3 _____
4 _____
5 _____
6 _____

2 Look and write. Write three things you need to make these things.

1 You need _____ to make a cake.
2 _____ puppet.
3 _____ letter.

1 Match and write.

Do your homework!   You must wear your raincoat!   Drink your milk!
Hurry up!   You must take your flask!   Eat your vegetables!

1 <u>If he hurries</u> _____ he won't be late.
2 _____ he won't be thirsty.
3 _____ he will be healthy.
4 _____ he won't get wet.
5 _____ he will pass the exam.
6 _____ his teeth will be strong.

2 Complete these sentences.

1 If _____, you will get wet.
2 If _____, you will feel hot.
3 If _____, you will feel cold.
4 If _____, your hat will blow off.

3 Look and finish the sentences.

✔✔   ✘   ✘   ✔   ✔   ✘

1 If you brush your teeth twice a day, you _____
2 _____, you will get hot.
3 _____ to the desert, _____

58   Unit 10   Lesson 2

1 If you mix these colours, what colours will you get?
If you like, you can colour the circles.

1 red   blue   If you mix red and blue, you will get _____.

2 yellow blue   _____.

3 white red   _____.

4 red   yellow _____.

5 white black   _____.

2 Do the sums and write sentences.

1 (15 + 7) _If you add 15 and 7, you will get_ _____

2 (12 − 5) _If you take 5 away from 12, you will get_ _____

3 (15 − 8) _____

4 (8 − 7)   _____

5 (12 + 9) _____

6 (9 + 5)   _____

7 (8 + 7)   _____

3 Draw and write. What will happen if you are late for school?
Draw a picture. Write a sentence about it.

Unit 10 Lesson 3

1 Write the words in the blocks.

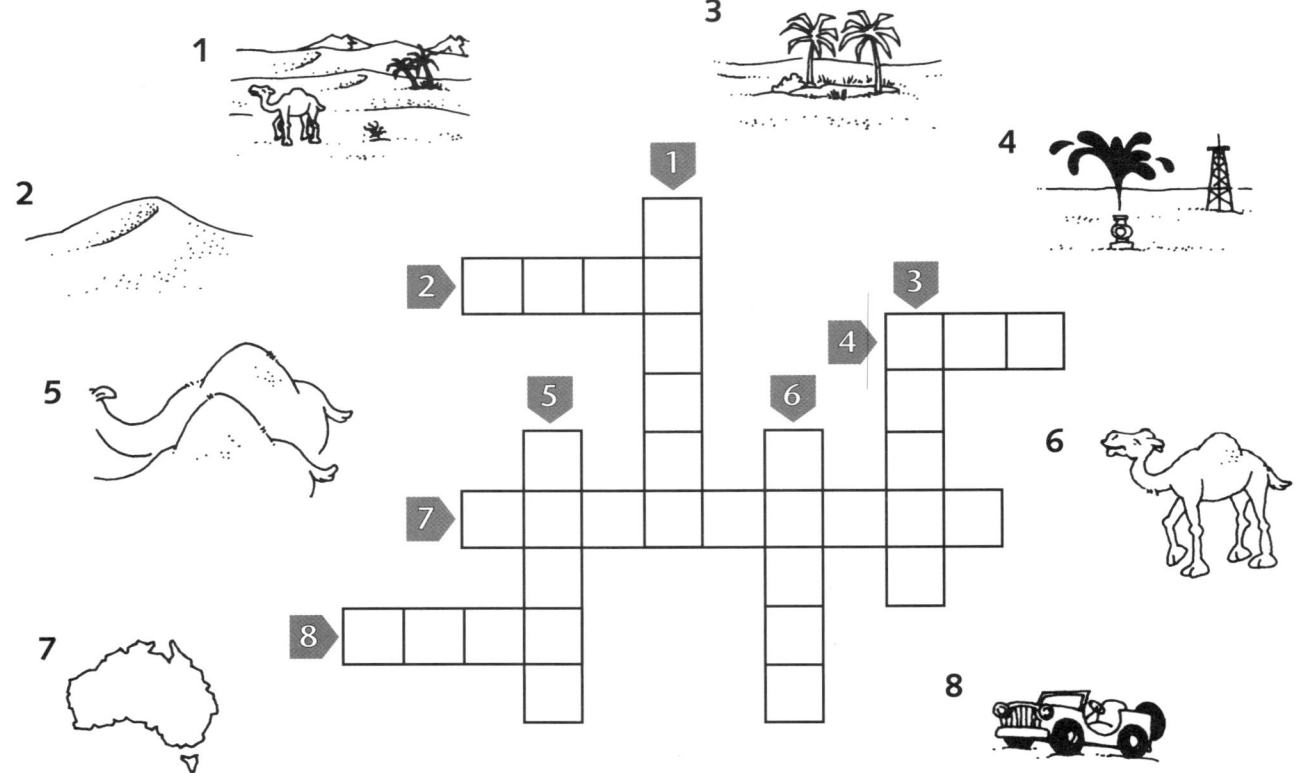

2 Write three sentences about a camel.

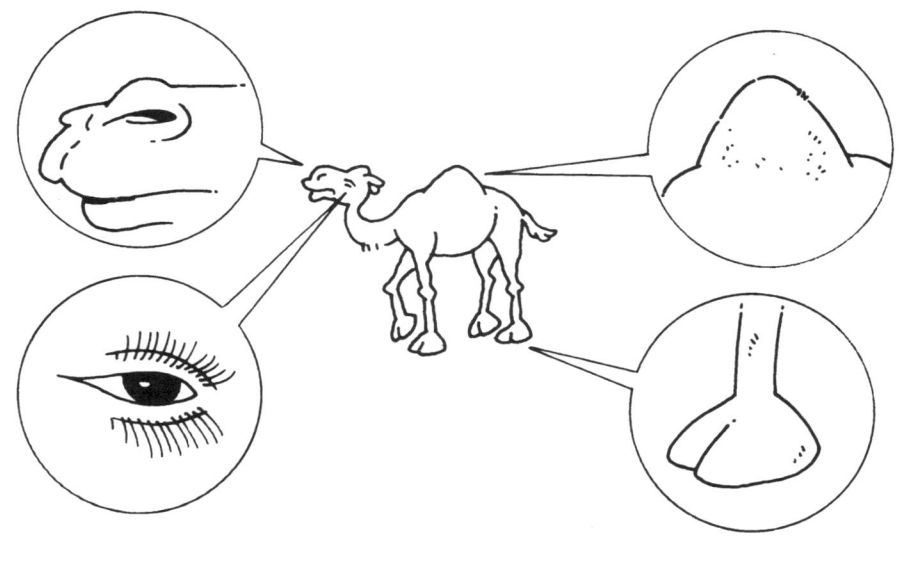

_____
_____
_____
_____

Composition

1 Last year Ibrahim lived in a town. Look and read.

This is Ibrahim. Last year he lived in a town. There were a lot of cars and taxis. It was noisy and dirty, but he liked it. Ibrahim lived in a large flat. He went to Palm Springs School. He liked his teacher very much. There was also a library. He went there after school. There were a lot of books. It was great! He sometimes went to the sports centre to swim and play tennis. On Saturdays he went to the cinema to watch the cartoons.

2 Now Ibrahim lives in the desert. Write about his life.

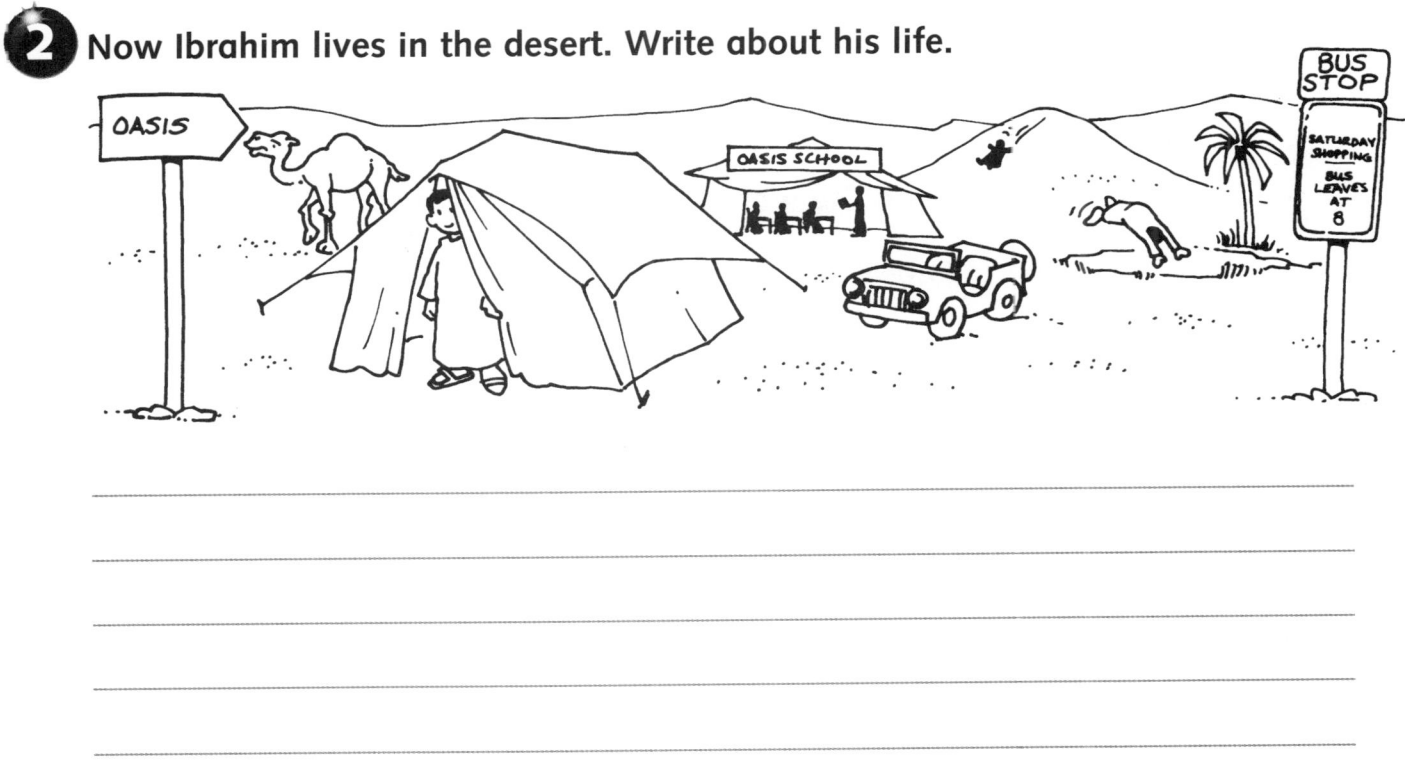

Unit 10 Composition

Study skills

1 Spelling.

Fill in the missing words.

| this | think | these | thank | thumb | thousand |

1. Whose books are _____?
2. Whose cap is _____?
3. _____ you for helping me.
4. David has cut his _____.
5. I _____ the answer is two _____.

Which word does not rhyme?

6 that   hate   flat   hat   _____
7 think   pink   sink   thank   _____
8 this   shirt   dirt   hurt   _____

2 Match the pictures with the words and their meanings.

1 ( ) noise   (1) the part of your face you use for smelling

2 (1) nose   ( ) a hard fruit in a hard shell

3 ( ) nothing   ( ) lots of loud sounds

4 ( ) nurse   ( ) someone who looks after sick people

5 ( ) nut   ( ) not even one thing

Unit 10 Study Skills

1 Match the people with their professions and say what they do.

1   ( ) A nurse   (1) fixes engines.

2   ( ) A pilot   ( ) helps people to learn.

3   ( ) A dentist   ( ) looks after sick people.

4   (1) A mechanic   ( ) flies planes.

5   ( ) A teacher   ( ) looks after people's teeth.

2 Fill in the missing words.

| air hostess | mechanics | check-in desk |
| plane | engines | suitcase | fly | ticket |

Mr Hill went on holiday by (1)_____ . At the (2)_____, they weighed his (3)_____. It was not very heavy. He gave his (4)_____ to the woman at the desk. She checked him in. Mr Hill saw the (5)_____ checking the plane's (6)_____. The pilot was ready to (7)_____ the plane. The (8)_____ showed Mr Hill to his seat.

3 Write two sentences about a plane.

Unit 11   Lesson 1   63

1 Write sentences. Use the words in the box.

| work at the ticket office | help the passengers | carry the suitcases |
| drive the train | sell sweets | work at the information desk |

1 He's the man who carries the suitcases.
2 _____
3 _____
4 _____
5 _____
6 _____

2 Who does these things? Write the professions. Write sentences.

fixes broken cars   looks after people on planes   looks after sick people   flies planes   makes bread

1 _____   2 _____   3 _____   4 _____   5 _____

1 A mechanic is a person who fixes broken cars.
2 _____
3 _____
4 _____
5 _____

Unit 11   Lesson 2

1 Read and circle.

Read the story. You choose the words.

When Mrs Blunt went to Disneyworld/ The Olympics,

she went in a / . It was her first/second time in a

plane. She was very excited/ scared.

'Don't worry/ be afraid,' said the air hostess. 'Everything

will be okay.'

'We may be late/ crash!' said Mrs Blunt.

'We won't / !' said the air hostess. 'The pilot is

very fast/good.' The plane ✗ / ✗.

Mrs Blunt wanted to fly/ did not want to fly again.

She went home by / .

2 Write your story about Mrs Blunt.

When Mrs Blunt _____

1 What do the people do? Match, then write sentences.

1 passengers	2 air hostess	3 nurses	4 mechanic	5 pilot	6 shopkeeper
D					

A	B	C	D	E	F
checks engines	work in hospital	sells things	go on planes	looks after passengers	flies a plane

1 Passengers are people who _____
2 An air hostess is a person that _____
3 _____
4 _____
5 _____
6 _____

2 Look and write sentences.

Woodside School
Class 4
Maths project: class survey
Exciting places in Clifton

puppet theatre	✓✓✓✓✓✓✓✓
zoo	✓✓✓✓✓
science museum	✓✓✓
aquarium	✓✓✓✓
funfair	✓✓✓✓✓✓✓✓✓
park	✓✓

more
less
most
least

exciting 1 The puppet theatre is _____ than the zoo.

2 The science museum is _____ than the aquarium.

3 The funfair is the _____ place.

4 The park is the _____ place.

Unit 11 Lesson 4

Composition

1 Yesterday Mat went on a plane. Look at the pictures. Write the numbers under the notes.

2 Write about Mat, using the notes.

Yesterday I

Study skills

1 Spelling.
Fill in the missing letters.

 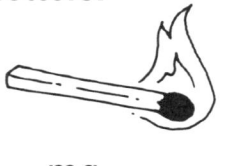  

wa _ _ _   ma _ _ _   ca _ _ _   fe _ _ _

Make words from these letters.

s c i t e s u a   k e t t c i   g e h i w

p r o i r a t   e e q u u   t i l o p

2 Write these sentences. Use . , ? and capital letters.

1 mr jones flew from london to cairo

   Mr Jones flew from London to Cairo.

2 when did mrs hill fly from paris to algiers

   _____

3 if becky goes to the sahara desert in may it will be hot

   _____

4 when emma went to spain on sunday she went by bus train and plane

   _____

5 why did uncle peter move from africa to the middle east

   _____

12

1 Look and write sentences.

What have they done? Use the words under the pictures.

1. (sail on) (be on) ✗   She has sailed on a boat.
   She hasn't been in a plane.

2. Clifton (go to) London (go to) ✗   She _____

3. (see) (live in) ✗   He _____

4. (go to) (go to) ✗   They _____

5. (go to) (walk across) ✗   They _____

6. (live in) (climb) ✗   He _____

2 Draw and write.

What have you done? Draw pictures and write sentences.

Unit 12 Lesson 1

1 Find the words and circle them, then ✔ the countries.
Bernie is a pilot. He has been to many places
and seen many things. Can you find them?

India   Germany   Egypt   Saudi Arabia   Australia   Morocco
☐   ☐   ☐   ☐   ☐   ☐

```
l  p  b  t  i  g  e  r  s  t
q  v  y  e  c  a  s  t  l  e
n  p  y  r  a  m  i  d  s  y
s  k  o  d  e  s  e  r  t  g
t  l  k  o  a  l  a  v  x  f
```

Bernie hasn't been to _____

2 Look and write.

1 Syria   4 Jordan
2 Iraq   5 Saudi Arabia
3 Egypt   6 Oman

1 Miss Pims has been to Syria, but Mr Jones hasn't.
2 Mr Jones has been to Iraq, but Miss Pims hasn't.
3 Mr Jones and Miss Pims have been to _____
4 Nobody has been to _____
5 _____
6 _____

Unit 12   Lesson 2

1 Look and write sentences.

I have seen a _____ but I haven't seen a _____.
I have seen a _____ and a _____.
_____.

Have you ever done these things?

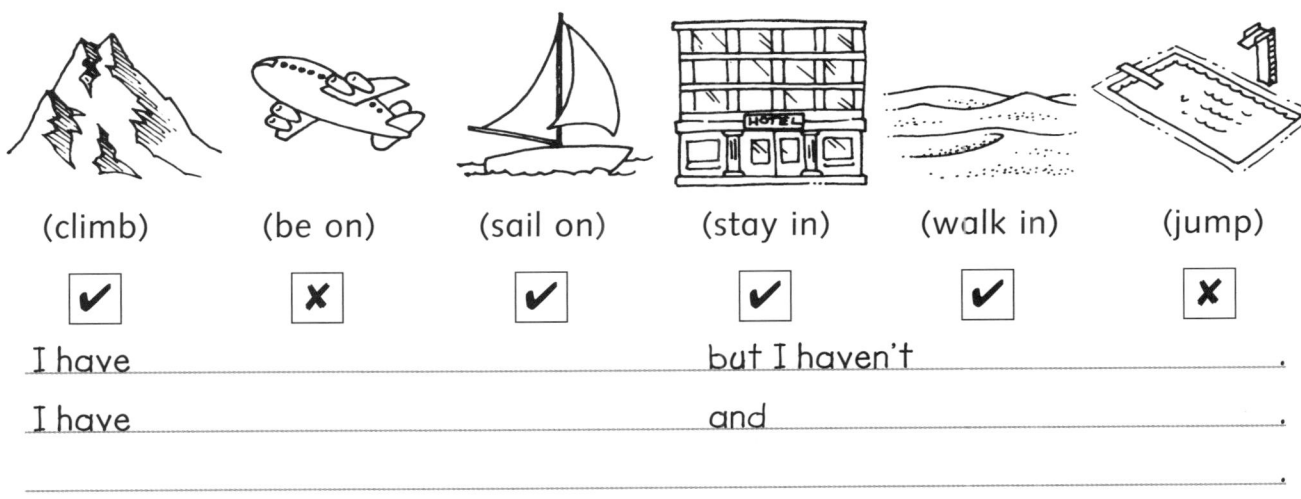

I have _____ but I haven't _____.
I have _____ and _____.
_____.

2 Have you ever been to these places?

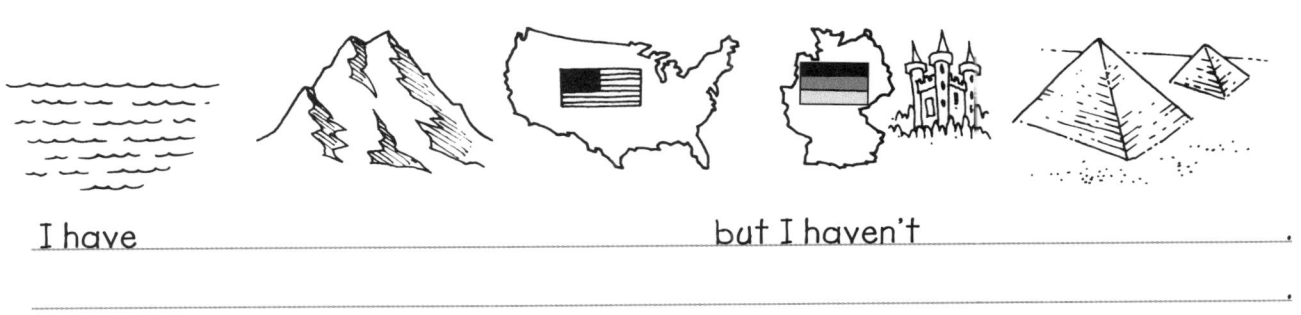

I have _____ but I haven't _____.
_____.

1 Write sentences. What does Grandmother make?

1. Grandmother makes delicious
2.
3.
4.
5.

What does Susie do to help Grandmother?

1. Susie does the
2.
3.
4.
5. Then

2 Draw and write. What do you make? What do you do to help?

Unit 12   Lesson 4

Composition

1 Look at the pictures. Complete the notes and write the letter.

| climbed | broken | been to | watched | seen |

Africa _____ _____ _____ _____

Dear Mike,

 I'm so sorry I haven't written to you for three months. I have been very busy. _____

_____

_____

I hope you are well. Have you been busy too? Write soon!

 Best wishes,
 From Pat

---

2 Read the notes and write the letter.

Dear Pat,

 Thank you for your letter. You have been busy! I have been busy, too.

_____

_____

_____

I hope your leg feels better.

been to desert
lived in tent
been to Germany
seen castle
climbed mountain

Unit 12 Composition 73

Study skills

1 Spelling.
Fill in the missing letters from the boxes.

| ar |
| op |
| ick |
| amp |

 st ___ ___    st ___ ___    st ___ ___    st ___ ___

| fa |
| lo |
| la |
| fir |

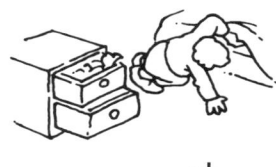 ___ ___ st    ___ ___ st    ___ ___ st    ___ ___ st

Which word does not rhyme?

stop	hop	mop	chop	chip	_____
star	bat	bar	car	jar	_____
snow	grow	green	toe	low	_____
higher	bear	pair	wear	hair	_____

Divide these words into syllables.

famous
desert
kangaroo
Australia
Egypt
Germany
pyramid
skyscraper
gorilla

fa | mous

Unit 12   Study Skills

13

1 Write sentences. What are they interested in?

Peter
collect ✔ Peter is interested in collecting stamps.
write ✘ He isn't interested in writing letters.

Sarah
bake ✔ _____
grow ✘ _____

Simon
play ✔ _____
make ✘ _____

Polly
read ✔ _____
riding ✘ _____

2 Make notes.

What are you interested in?  Your friend?  Your teacher?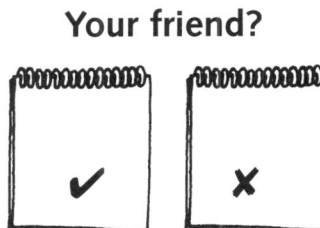

Write sentences.

_____
_____
_____
_____

Unit 13 Lesson 1

1 Look and write sentences.

1. This book is interesting. _____
2. This game is boring. _____
3. Computers _____) He is bored.
4. This film _____) She is excited.
5. Roller blading _____) They _____
6. Science _____
7. Sailing _____
8. This letter _____

2 Write sentences about something that is exciting, something that is boring and something that is interesting.

I think _____

Composition

1 Read and ✔. Read these emails from internet friends. Which things are in both emails? In one email?

name   country   lives in   hobbies   loves/likes

I'm Chang. I'm from China. I live in Beijing. Beijing is a very large city. I like Beijing but I also love the sea. Last summer I went to the seaside. My uncle is a fisherman and we went fishing. It was very exciting because we used a kite! Here is a picture.

kite fishing

I'm Alice, from the USA. I live on a farm in the mountains. I would like a pal who collects stamps. I have a very interesting stamp collection. I collect stamps from all over the world. I also like horses. I am bored because I am the only child here. Please email soon!

a mountain farm

2 Write an email to Chang or Alice. Be sure to write the things with two ✔s. Choose an ending from Chang or Alice's email.

Unit 13 Composition (Lesson 3) 77

Study skills

1 Spelling.
Fill in the missing words.

> quick quiet question
> queen quiz queue

1 We stood in a _____ to buy tickets.

2 Jack asked his teacher a _____ .

3 Sarah knew all the answers in the _____ .

4 We must keep _____ in the classroom.

5 Be _____ , or you will miss the bus!

6 The king and the _____ lived in the castle.

2 Finish these sentences.

> Australia Egypt Africa Russia
> Spain Lebanon England Turkey

1 Spanish people come from _____ .

2 Lebanese people come from the _____ .

3 English people come from _____ .

4 Turkish people come from _____ .

5 Egyptians come from _____ .

6 Australians come from _____ .

7 Africans come from _____ .

8 Russians come from _____ .

3 Find the odd one out.

1	Australia	England	London	Egypt	Spain	_____
2	mountain	tent	river	forest	desert	_____
3	plane	bus	train	bicycle	chair	_____

Unit 13 Study Skills

Revision

1 Complete the sentences using the information. Write the numbers in full
(496 – four hundred and ninety six)

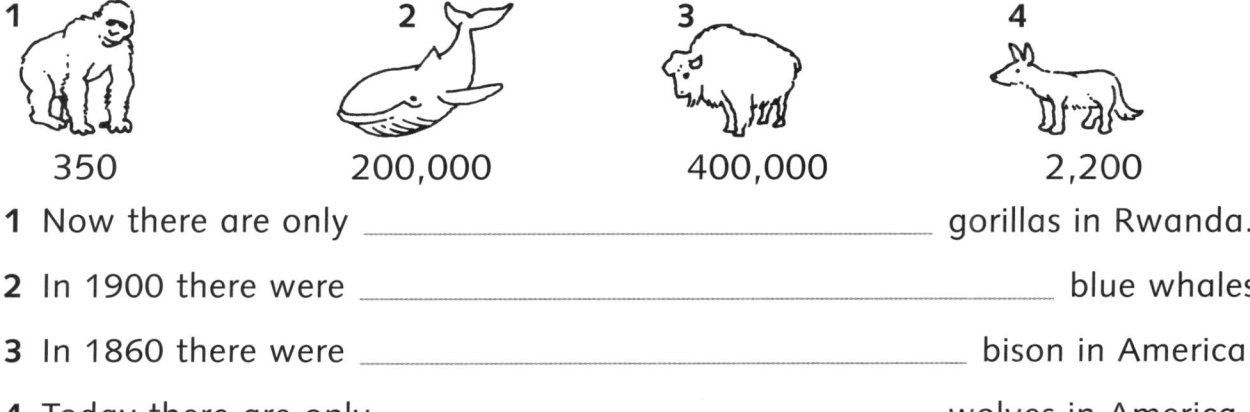

1	2	3	4
350	200,000	400,000	2,200

1 Now there are only _____ gorillas in Rwanda.

2 In 1900 there were _____ blue whales.

3 In 1860 there were _____ bison in America.

4 Today there are only _____ wolves in America.

2 Write sentences about the zoo. Use words from the boxes.

| water | trees | people | gorillas | monkeys |

| only a few | only a little | lots of |

1 _____

2 _____

3 _____

4 _____

5 _____

3 Look at the words and pictures. Then answer the questions.

1 What do you need to make a cake? _____
2 What do you need to be warm? _____
3 What do you need to make a fire? _____
4 What does a reporter need for his work? _____

4 Write about these places. Use the words 'If you go to … you'll …' Use the words in the box.

| eat   see   need |

London   China   Rwanda

1 _____
2 _____
3 _____

5 Write answers. ✔ 'Yes, I …' ✘ 'No, I …'

1 'Have you ever been to Japan?'   ✘
_____

2 'Have you ever climbed a mountain?'   ✔
_____

3 'Have you finished the dishes?'   ✔
_____

4 'Have you seen some tigers?'   ✘
_____

Unit 13 Revision continued

14

1 Look and write the words.

High Top   Clifton

1 _____ has more 🔺 _____ than _____ .

2 _____ has fewer 👜 _____ than _____ .

3 _____ has less ❄ _____ than _____ .

4 _____ has fewer 🧍 _____ than _____ .

5 _____ has more 🏠 _____ than _____ .

2 Write sentences. Use 'more, fewer, less'.

1 Ned   Ned has more sweets than Sam.   Sam

2 Cath   _____   Jenny

3 Tom   _____   Jim

4 Jane   _____   Meg

5 Mike   _____   Jim

Unit 14 Lesson 1   81

1 Write the words in the boxes.

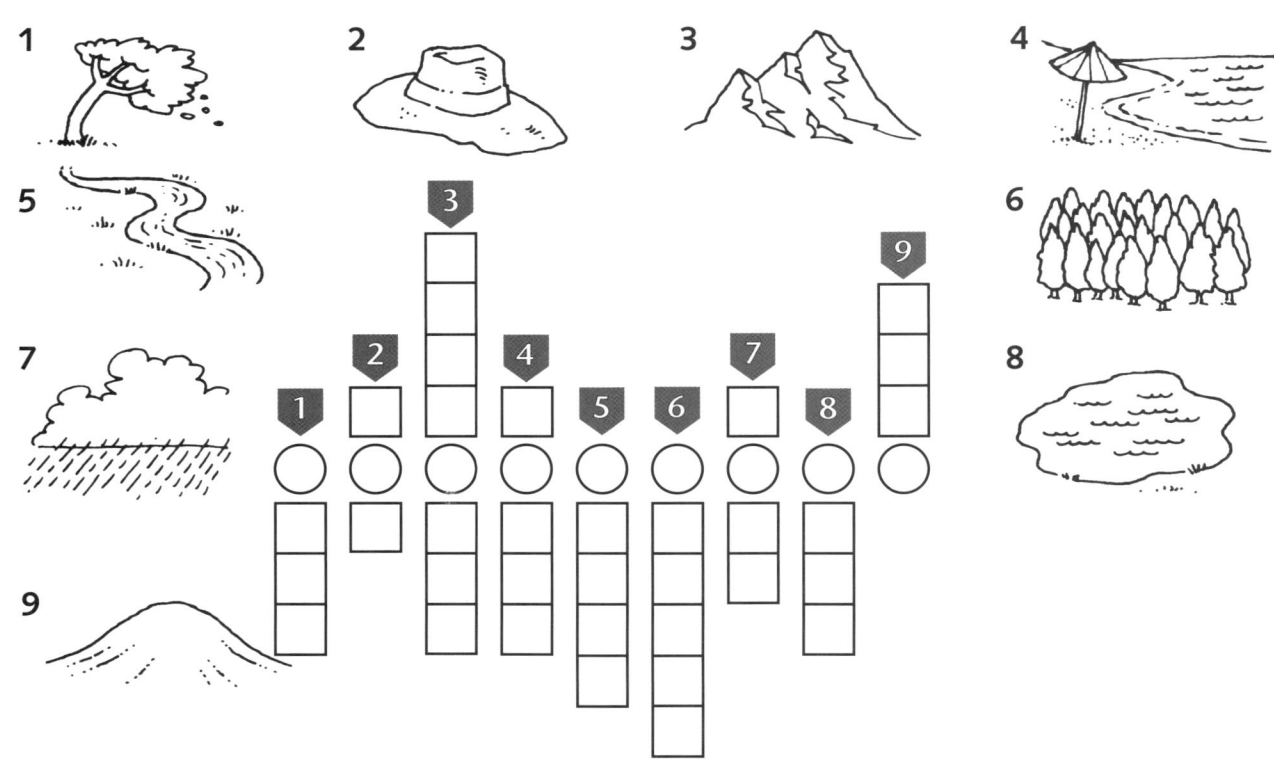

Write the word in the circles. _____

2 Look and write.

1 _____ has the most sun.

2 _____ has the least rain.

3 _____ has fewer mountains than Green Island.

4 Sunny Island _____ mountains.

5 _____ has the most mountains.

6 North Island _____ sun.

82 Unit 14 Lesson 2

1 Read and write the names.

Where does Anna sit at the table? Where do John and Peg sit?

Anna eats lots of fruit. She eats it every day. She also drinks lots of milk. She only eats a few sweets. She usually has a little bread and some cheese.

John loves sweet things. He eats lots of sweets. But he eats some fruit and drinks some milk, too. He eats lots of bread, but he only eats a little cheese.

Peg drinks a little milk. She doesn't eat very much. She eats some bread and a lot of cheese. She eats some sweets and she eats a little fruit, too.

2 Answer the questions.

1 Who eats fewer sweets, John or Peg? _____
2 Who drinks more milk, Anna or John? _____
3 Who eats less bread, Peg or Anna? _____
4 Who eats the most bread? _____
5 Who eats the fewest apples? _____
6 Who drinks the least milk? _____

1 The children are starting a project about winter. They are going to write about a place with cold weather. They have this information. What are they saying? Use the words in the box.

Russia	North America	North Pole

more
less
fewer
most
least
fewest

1 I want to write about Russia, because it has _____ bears than North America, and it has the _____ forests.

2 I want to write about the North Pole because it has the _____ ice and it has _____ snow than Russia.

3 But the North Pole has the _____ bears and the _____ sun! I want to write about North America because it has the _____ mountains and the _____ lakes.

4 But North America has _____ bears than Russia and it has _____ snow.

5 Russia has _____ ice than North America, too. Let's write about Russia!

2 Write sentences.

North America/The North Pole 🐻 <u>North America has more bears than the North Pole.</u>

North America 🧊 <u>North America has the least ice.</u>

1 North America/Russia 🌲 _____

2 North Pole ⛰ _____

3 Russia/North America ☀ _____

4 North Pole/Russia 🌲🌲🌲 _____

5 Russia/North America ❄ _____

84 Unit 14 Lesson 4

Composition

1 Read and draw. Lisa went to an island on holiday.
Look at her postcard. Draw something she saw on the front.

Hi Sue!

I'm having a wonderful time here on Sunny Island. On Monday I climbed a very high mountain and I saw a waterfall. On Tuesday I saw some beautiful lakes and had a picnic in a very dark forest. Yesterday I went to the beach. It's very hot here and I'm sunburnt!

From
Lisa

2 Write a postcard. Look at the picture and use the notes.

saw mountain
very tall/snow

sailed on river
windy/scared

Blue Mountains

waterfall/
big/noisy

forest/
dark/scary

Dear _____
I'm having a _____ time _____

Unit 14   Composition

Study skills

1 **Spelling.**

Say these words. The <u>i</u> has a short sound.

pin   bit   win   pip   hid

Say these words. The <u>i</u> has a long sound.

pine   bite   wine   pipe   hide

Use the words in the boxes to complete the sentences.

| pin | pine |

Sam found a _____ under the _____ tree.

| pip | pipe |

Grandpa sat on a _____ when he was smoking his _____.

| bit | bite |

Emma _____ her lip when she tried to _____ the apple.

| hid | hide |

Ned told Jack to _____, so he _____ behind the tree.

2 **Write sentences. Remember the '.**

1 This pipe belongs to Grandpa.   <u>It's Grandpa's pipe.</u>
   <u>It's his.</u>

2 This book belongs to Emma.

3 This money belongs to Mum.

4 This ticket belongs to Dad.

5 This camel belongs to Ibrahim.

15

1 Write the words in the boxes.

2 Write sentences about this picture. Use the words in the box.

| sold | talked | mended | fished | sailed | caught |

When the weather was good,
_____
_____
_____

Unit 15   Lesson 1   **87**

1 What happened yesterday?

Make notes under each picture. Use the words in the box.

| lots of fish/happy | cat came/stole/fish |
| fishmonger chased | other cats/came/ate | very angry |

A ☐

B ☐

C ☐

D ☐

Put the pictures in order. Write the numbers in the boxes.

2 Finish the story.

Mr Scampi is a fishmonger. He has a shop in the market. Yesterday _____

While he was standing _____

While he was chasing the cat _____

88 Unit 15   Lesson 2

1 Match and write.

This is Fiona's day. Write the words next to the pictures.

| playing | eating | doing | watching | reading | having |
| the piano | lunch | homework | TV | a story | a bath |

1.00
2.30
3.30
5.00
7.00
9.00

This is Jim's day. Write words next to the times.

| playing | eating | playing | watching | doing | playing |
| with Fred | chips | computer games | TV | homework | football |

1.00
2.30
3.30
5.00
7.00
9.00

2 Write sentences about Jim and Fiona.

1 While Fiona was eating lunch,
2 While Jim was   , Fiona was watching TV.
3
4
5
6

Unit 15   Lesson 3   89

1 **Yesterday was a holiday. What were John and Karen doing? Write sentences.**

1 While John was reading, Karen was sleeping.
2 _____
3 _____
4 _____
5 _____
6 _____

2 **Complete the sentences. Use the words in the box.**

| more | most | less | least |

exciting

1 A looks _____ than B.
2 C looks _____ than B.
3 C looks the _____.
4 A looks the _____.

boring

1 A is the _____.
2 C is the _____.
3 B is _____ than A.
4 A is _____ than B.

Composition

1 Look and read.

Read this story and look at the pictures. Are they in the right order?

A _____. He loved fishing. Yesterday he went to the river to fish. He waited and waited, but he didn't catch a fish.

B _____. He ate a sandwich, and another sandwich, and another sandwich. Then he ate some cake.

C _____. The sun was very hot. Mickey fell asleep. While he was sleeping, a very big fish took the line. Whoops! Mickey was very wet. But he still didn't have a fish!

2 Choose sentences for A, B and C. Write them on the lines.

A Mickey was twelve years old.   Mickey was a fisherman.   This is Mickey.
B Mickey was hungry.   Mickey was angry.   Mickey likes cake.
C He wanted to watch TV.   Again Mickey waited.   He wasn't hungry.

3 Write the end of the story. This is what happened next. Put the sentences in order.

a Mickey climbed out of the water. ☐
c What a funny way to catch a fish! ☐
e It was jumping out of the water. ☐
b He wasn't very happy. ☐
d It landed in Mickey's net! ☐
f Then he saw the fish! ☐

Unit 15 Composition

Study skills

1 Spelling.

Read these words. The o has a short sound.

hop   rod   not

Read these words. The o has a long sound.

hope   rode   note

Which word does not rhyme?

hope	rope	hop	pope	_____
rode	odd	load	toad	_____
hot	boat	note	coat	_____
pole	foal	stole	fell	_____
loss	nose	rose	toes	_____

2 Quickly look for the numbers in these sentences. Write them.

1 There were 20,000 gorillas once.   <u>twenty thousand</u>

2 Our school has 680 pupils.   _____

3 The sale will begin on 26th January.   _____

4 The train leaves at 8.30 from
   platform 13.   _____

5 My brother is turning 21 on
   18th February.   _____

6 There were 500,000 passenger pigeons.   _____

Now go back and read the sentences slowly and carefully.

16

1 What will happen in the future?

Answer the questions. Use the answers in the box.

| Yes, I will.   Perhaps I may.   No, I won't. |

Life in the future – What do you think?

1 Will you go to the moon? _____

2 Will you have a job? _____

3 Will you go to university? _____

4 Will you travel around the world? _____

5 Will you get married? _____

6 Will you have children? _____

7 Will you have lots of friends? _____

8 Will you live in a castle? _____

2 Write three sentences about you in the future.

1 I will _____

2 I may _____

3 I won't _____

Unit 16   Lesson 1

1 What's wrong?
Make words from the letters to find out. Write sentences.

1. t h o — It's too hot!
2. i n y s o — _____
3. g b i — _____
4. a r d k — _____
5. d e r c o d w — _____
6. a n d r e g s o u — _____
7. g h h i — _____
8. f o s t — _____

2 Write questions.

1. ✗ Why didn't Jack go swimming?   Because it was too cold.
2. ✗ _____   Because it was too hot.
3. ✗ _____   Because it was too boring.
4. ✗ _____   Because it was too heavy.
5. ✗ _____   Because it was too sweet.
6. ✗ _____   Because it was too hot.

Unit 16 Lesson 2

1 What will I become?

Write sentences about Peter.

Peter may become _____   He won't _____

2 What will I do after school?

Write sentences about Mary.

Mary may bake a cake after school. She won't _____

1 Read and find.

Read the fact file. Write the numbers under the pictures.

Space

1 John Glenn was the first American in space.
2 Russia sent the first rocket into space.
3 The name of the first animal in space was Laika.
4 The first satellite weighed eighty-three kilograms.
5 The Russian astronaut went round the world once.
6 This was the speed of Glenn's spacecraft: twenty-eight thousand kilometres an hour

That's fast!

2 Read and write the words.

On October 4, 1957, _____ put its first satellite into space. It was called Sputnik 1 and it weighed _____ . One month later the Russians put another satellite into space. This satellite carried the world's first space traveller, a dog called _____ .

Three and a half years later, in April 1961, Yuri Gagarin from Russia went round the world _____ in a satellite. He was the first man to fly in space.

These satellites fly fast. When John Glenn was the first _____ to fly in space round the world, his spacecraft was travelling at _____ kilometres an hour only five minutes after it left the earth.

Composition

1 Look at the picture. Your life may be like this in the future. Draw your own idea.

2 Look and write. Write about life in the future. Use 'may' or 'may not' and the words in the box.

| travel to | eat | wear | live in | buy |

_____
_____
_____
_____

Unit 16 Composition

Study skills

1 Spelling.
Fill in the missing letters.

 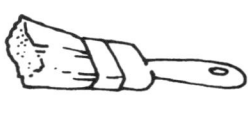 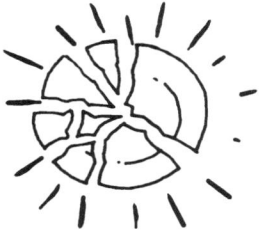 

br __ __ __   br __ __ __   br __ __ __ __   br __ __ __

Make words from these letters.

natlep   ensarubmi   rhapaucet

_____   _____   _____

2 Match the pictures with the words and their meanings.

1    ( ) brave   ( ) a woman getting married

2    ( ) breathe   ( ) not afraid

3    ( ) bride   ( ) the colour of chocolate

4    ( ) bridge   ( ) take air into your body

5    ( ) brown   ( ) a road over a river

3 Write these sentences. Use , . ' ' ? and capital letters.

1 ben said my father is very brave because he isn't afraid of snakes
2 sam said we are going to a wedding on tuesday and my cousin meg is the bride
3 andy asked when we go to cairo will we see a bridge over the river nile
4 the firefighter said if there is smoke in the house it will be difficult to breathe

17

1 Write answers.

1. What will Betty have for dinner?
   Betty will have either meat or fish for dinner.

2.  What will Sam play tomorrow?

3. What will the weather be like tomorrow?

4.  What will Becky put in her tea?

5.  Where will Jack go next year?

6.  What will Mrs Smith wear tonight?

7.  How will we travel to Spain?

8.  What will Ned buy at the department store?

9.  What will Emma give her mother?

10.  Where will Nina stay on her holiday?

Unit 17   Lesson 1

1 Name these things. Then find the words in the puzzle and circle them.

1 _____ 2 _____ 3 _____ 4 _____

5 _____ 6 _____ 7 _____ 8 _____

```
k v (s e a g u l l) x o
m p  e x n j e s y s e
c m  a s t b p u k z i
r f  w a v e s r c j a
a i  e s t a r f i s h
b y  e t s h r e m t q
u h  d u g e s r o c k
f e  a t h e r g t i y
```

2 Look and write sentences. You are going to the seaside for your holiday. What will you do and see?

_____
_____
_____
_____
_____
_____
_____

1 Look and write.

Jane likes making these things. What will she use?

1. She will use flour and sugar to make a cake.
2. _____
3. _____
4. _____
5. _____
6. _____

2 Find, circle and write.

How many things can you find that we can make? Circle the words.

dollkitepuppetfirecakedresspictureshirtgamedrawingsweetsmaskbiscuitsbread

What do you make? Write a sentence about something you make.

_____

_____

Unit 17   Lesson 3   101

1 Look and write. Look at the pictures and ✔ or ✘.
Then write sentences. Use 'will' and 'won't'.
We want to look after our seashores!

1. look for — We will look for shells.
2. have
3. leave
4. take
5. pick
6. touch
7. go

2 Write a sentence about each picture. Use 'won't be able'.

1.
2.
3.

Composition

1 Look at the pictures. Can you remember the story? Make more notes.

Who? _____
Where? _____
What? <u>seagull/black stuff/feathers</u>

What was it? _____
Where did it come from? _____
How did they feel? _____

Who? _____
What did she do? _____

Who wanted to help? _____
What did they do on Saturday? _____
_____

2 Write the story.

<u>Last summer</u> _____

_____

_____

_____

_____

Unit 17 Composition 103

Study skills

1 Spelling.
Fill in the missing letters.

 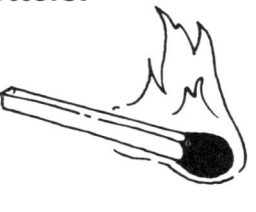  

_ _ _ ch   _ _ _ ch   _ _ _ ch   _ _ ch

Write words that rhyme.

goat    _____   _____

sea   _____   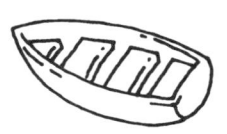 _____

mine   _____   

2 Write these sentences. Use , ' ' ? and capital letters.

1 sarah asked have you ever been to portugal

   <u>Sarah asked, 'Have you ever been to Portugal?'</u>

2 peter asked has mr jones been to cairo

_____

3 emma asked is jenny your sister

_____

4 mum asked have you given paul the present

_____

5 mr hill asked have you been to south america

_____

18

1 Look at Mrs Jones in her kitchen. What does she have to do?

2 Look and match. Make sentences about Mrs Jones.

1 She has to pick up the broken glass   ( ) so that they won't get dirty.
2 She has to put the meat in the fridge   ( ) so that it won't burn.
3 She has to put the ice cream in the freezer ( ) so that nobody will step on it.
4 She has to feed the baby   ( ) so that the cat won't eat it.
5 She has to put the books away   ( ) so that she doesn't waste water.
6 She has to put the flowers in water   ( ) so that it won't melt.
7 She has to take the cake out of the oven   ( ) so that they won't die.
8 She has to turn off the tap   ( ) so that he will stop crying.

3 Look and write. What do we have to do to keep our beaches clean and safe? Complete the sentences.

1 We have to _____
   so that _____

2 _____
   so that _____

Unit 18   Lesson 1   105

1 Look, find and write sentences.

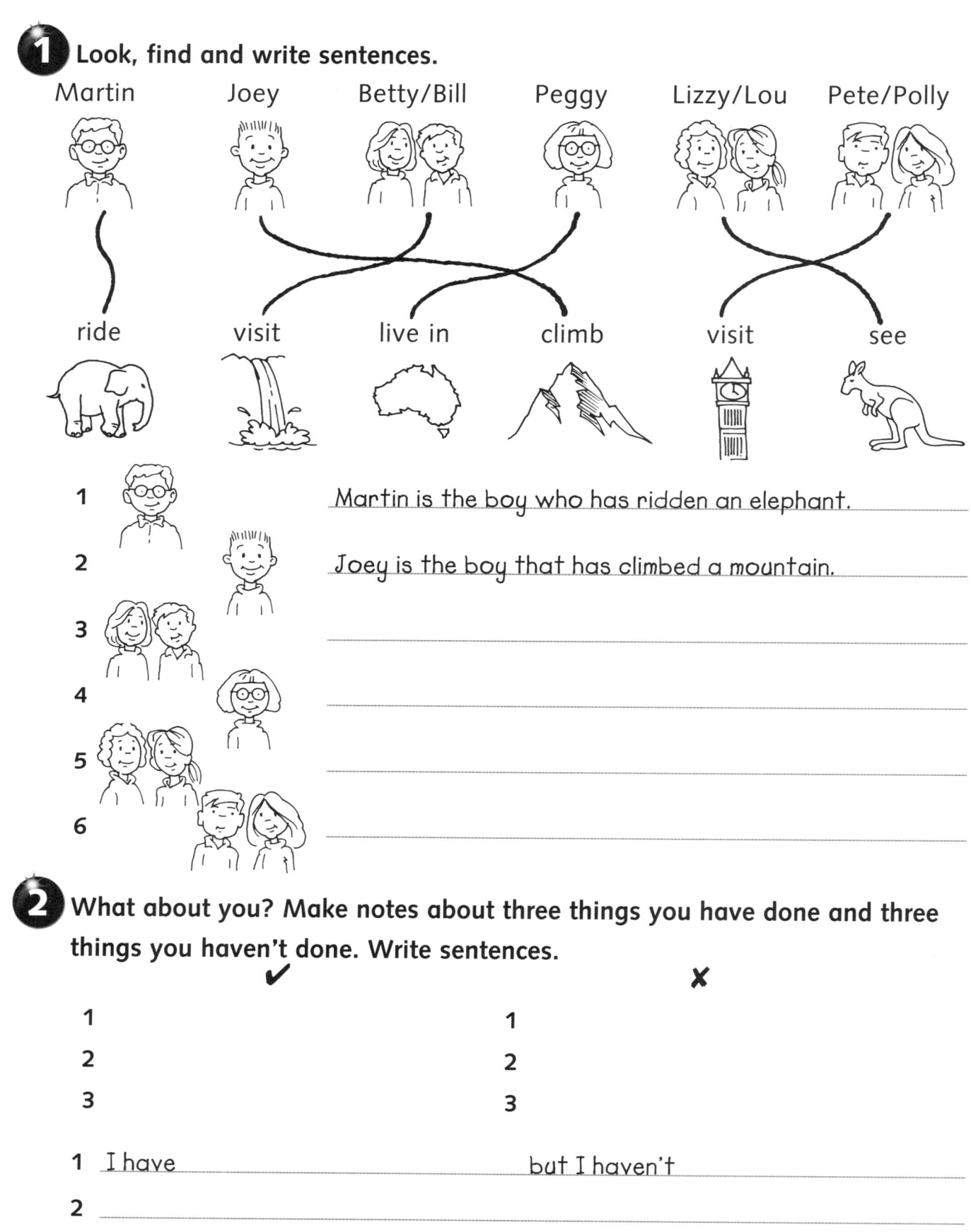

1 Martin is the boy who has ridden an elephant.
2 Joey is the boy that has climbed a mountain.
3 _____
4 _____
5 _____
6 _____

2 What about you? Make notes about three things you have done and three things you haven't done. Write sentences.

✔
1
2
3

✘
1
2
3

1 I have _____ but I haven't _____
2 _____
3 _____

Unit 18   Lesson 2

Composition

1 Do you remember Jack?

Look at the pictures and read the words.

go by train
live in

puppet factory
cut out clothes

toothache
Beck's father
dentist

late to school
Mrs Hill
happy

father   work
desert   water
flask

help   seagull
beach   oil
feathers

2 Write about Jack.

_____
_____
_____
_____
_____
_____
_____

Study skills

1 Spelling.
Write words that rhyme.

soap _____

nose _____

star _____

hair _____

cat _____

pink _____

talk _____

height _____

feed _____

2 Find the odd one out.

1 Cairo   London   France   Rome   _____
2 gorilla kangaroo horse   pigeon   _____
3 space   school   planet   moon   _____
4 bicycle cinema   theatre   restaurant _____

3 Put these words in alphabetical order.

1 bread   fruit   eggs   banana   meat   vegetables

_____

2 bus   train   plane   boat   bicycle   car

_____

Unit 18 Study Skills

Revision

1 Write about the different places below. Use the words in the box.

A   B   C

1 A and B have _____ snow than C.
2 A has the _____ sun.
3 B has the _____ people than C.
4 C has the _____ people, sun and snow.
5 A has the _____ people.

> least
> most
> fewer
> less
> fewest

2 What are their hobbies? Write sentences.

1 *I collect stamps.*   Her hobby is _____.
2 *I play tennis.*   _____
3 *We roller blade.*   _____
4 *I learn Chinese.*   _____

3 What have they done? Write sentences. Use the words in the box.

| stayed | looked | made | been | climbed |

1 We've _____
2 I've _____
3 _____
4 _____
5 _____

Unit 18 Revision   109

4 Use 'either' and 'or'. Use the words in the box.

| ride | be | I'll have | it will |

1  _____

2  _____

3  _____

4 _____

5 Write about what may and will happen tomorrow.

1 Ned  _____

_____

2 Emma  _____

_____

3 Jack  _____

_____

6 Write answers with 'too'. Use the words in the brackets.

1 Why didn't Jack go to school?  _____
(ill)

2 Why didn't they eat the soup? _____
(hot)

3 Why did they go to sleep?  _____
(boring)

Verbs

Look at this!

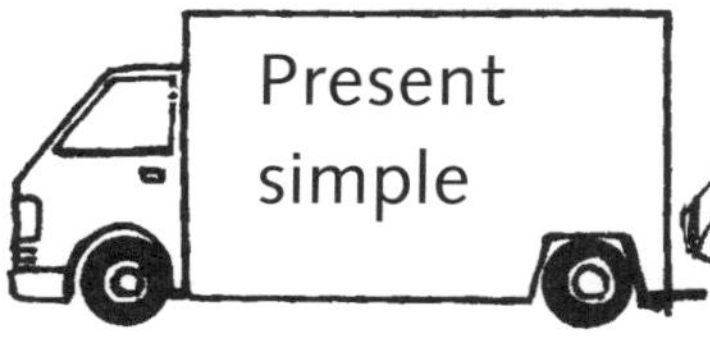

Present simple

I work	We work
You work	You work
He work**s**	They work
She work**s**	
It work**s**	

Present continuous

I am work**ing**	*We are* work**ing**
You are work**ing**	*You are* work**ing**
He is work**ing**	*They are* work**ing**
She is work**ing**	
It is work**ing**	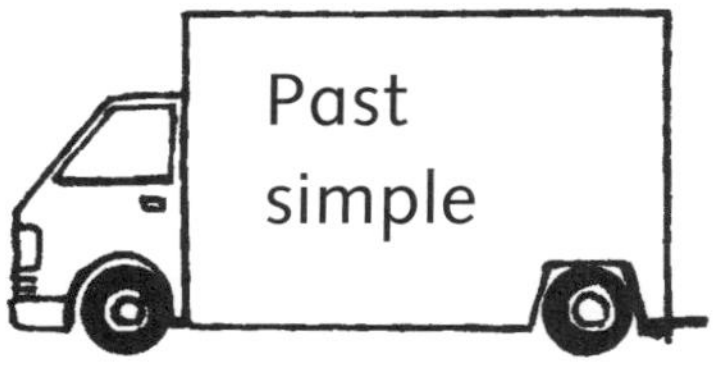

Past simple

I work**ed**	We work**ed**
You work**ed**	You work**ed**
He work**ed**	They work**ed**
She work**ed**	
It work**ed**	

Past continuous

I was work**ing**	*We were* work**ing**
You were work**ing**	*You were* work**ing**
He was work**ing**	*They were* work**ing**
She was work**ing**	
It was work**ing**	

Present perfect

I have worked	We have worked
You have worked	You have worked
He has worked	They have worked
She has worked	
It has worked	

Future (going to)

I am going to work	We are going to work
You are going to work	You are going to work
He is going to work	They are going to work
She is going to work	
It is going to work	

Future (will)

I will work	We will work
You will work	We will work
He will work	They will work
She will work	
It will work	

First conditional

If I work, *I'll* …	If we work, *we'll* …
If you work, *you'll* …	If you work, *you'll* …
If he works, *he'll* …	If they work, *they'll* …
If she works, *she'll* …	
If it works, *it'll* …	

Verbs